David L. Mowery

Morgan's Great Raid

The Remarkable Expedition from Kentucky to Ohio

9/28/13

Dear Jeanie & Marshall,

Thanks you for your interest in the Civil War and in Morgan's Raid. I'm so glad to know you through N.E.W. I hope you enjoy the book!

Charleston · London

THE History PRESS

All the best,

David L. Mowery

Published by The History Press
Charleston, SC 29403
www.historypress.net

Cover image: From the original painting by Mort Künstler, *Morgan's Ohio Raid*. © 2003
Mort Künstler, Inc. www.mkunstler.com.

First published 2013
Second printing 2013

Manufactured in the United States

ISBN 978.1.60949.436.0

Library of Congress CIP data applied for.

Notice: The information in this book is true and complete to the best of our knowledge. It is
offered without guarantee on the part of the author or The History Press. The author and
The History Press disclaim all liability in connection with the use of this book.

For my parents, who fueled the flame inside me

and

For my wife, who helped me to keep it burning

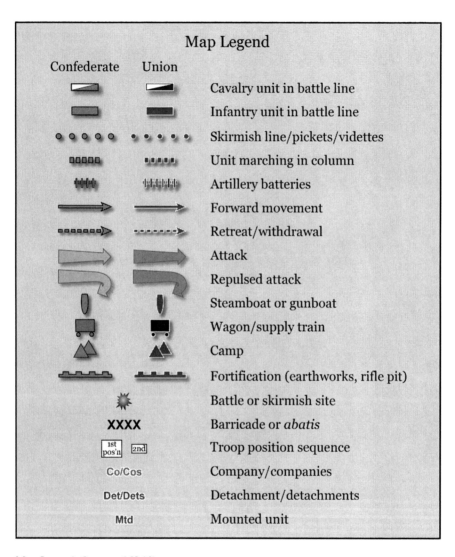

Map Legend. *Courtesy of Hal Jespersen.*

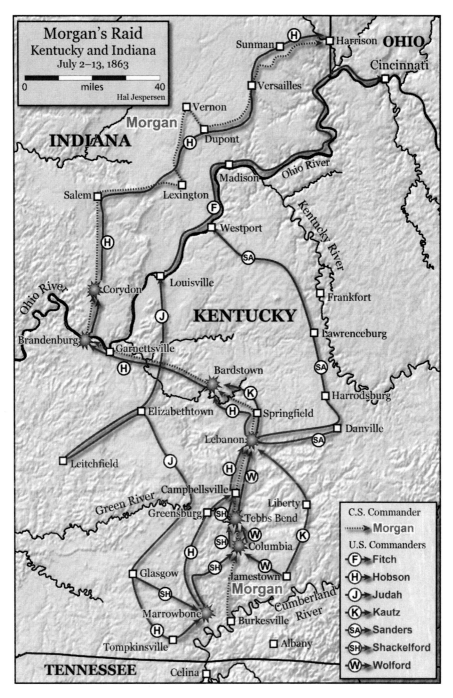

Map of Morgan's Great Raid in Kentucky and Indiana. *Author's collection.*

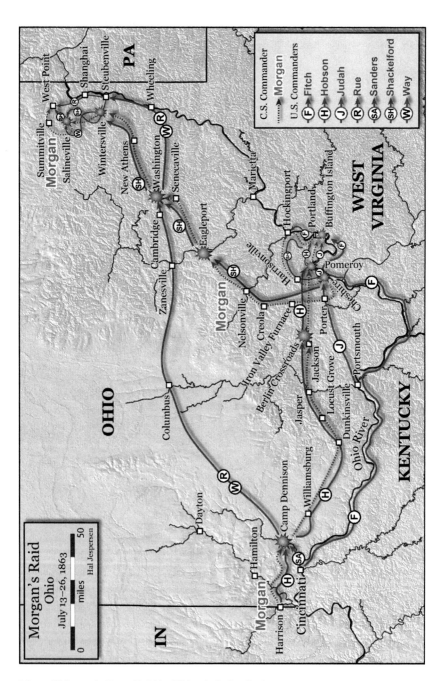

Map of Morgan's Great Raid in Ohio. *Author's collection.*

Contents

List of Maps

Preface

W hy did a young American woman label an enemy's raid "one of the most remarkable expeditions in military history" at a time when women's opinions didn't really matter? How dare she! She had absolutely no military training or experience. She gleaned no conclusions from a previous military advisor or author. Military judgment was reserved for men, not women. Was this girl misguided? Was she an enemy sympathizer? Was she nuts? None of the above. On the contrary, this woman proved to be exceptionally brilliant.

Miss Flora E. Simmons published the first overview of one of America's greatest military achievements: John Hunt Morgan's Great Raid. Her self-published book, *A Complete Account of the John Morgan Raid through Kentucky, Indiana and Ohio, in July 1863*, hit the public venues within three months after the raid had ended. Simmons unknowingly possessed a natural aptitude for the art of war. She looked past the final result of Morgan's Raid and saw its innovative qualities. While many of America's military experts of her day, both Union and Confederate, scoffed at Morgan's disastrous offensive, Simmons realized its value for generations of warriors to come. "Nothing could exceed the energy as well as skill and celerity of Morgan's movements, except perhaps the troops sent in pursuit of him," she concluded.

Historians and military experts who have come after her would agree. Those like J.F.C. Fuller, Heinz Guderian and Basil Henry Liddell Hart, the pioneers of mechanized warfare, realized the practical application of Morgan's raiding tactics. The swift movement of infantry and artillery deep into enemy territory, with as much stealth and deception as possible, are common characteristics of today's warfare. The Blitzkrieg, Operation Iraqi Freedom and even Operation Neptune Spear are appropriate examples. In 1863, this style of warfare was revolutionary, and many thought it unlawful.

From July 2 through July 26, 1863, Confederate brigadier general John Hunt Morgan led a division of approximately 2,460 cavalrymen and a battery of four guns from Burkesville, Kentucky, to West Point, Ohio, on a one-thousand-mile raid designed to divert Union forces away from Tennessee. Known interchangeably as the Indiana-Ohio Raid, the Ohio Raid or the Great Raid, Morgan's incursion into Union-held western Kentucky, southern Indiana and southern and eastern Ohio marked the pinnacle of Morgan's career, but it led to the destruction of one of the South's greatest cavalry divisions. When General Morgan surrendered near West Point on July 26, he had with him 364 men and officers from the original 2,460. No more than 500 men of the division successfully reached Confederate lines.

Nevertheless, Morgan's Great Raid falls on the list of groundbreaking military achievements in world history, not for its outcome, but for its execution. Even today, historians who study modern raiding techniques revere Morgan's Indiana-Ohio Raid. For example, Samuel A. Southworth's book *Great Raids in History: From Drake to Desert One* (Edison, NJ: Castle Books, 2002) lists Morgan's Ohio Raid as one of the top eighteen greatest land-based military raids in world history since the time of Sir Francis Drake's raid on Cadiz in 1587.

The innovator behind the Indiana-Ohio Raid was a unique man in his own right. John Hunt Morgan had not been trained at West Point, the Virginia Military Institute or any other academy. He was a Southern aristocrat who had seen brief action with a cavalry unit during the Mexican-American War. That experience alone did not make him a brilliant commander. What defined Morgan as a special military leader were his independent nature, his quick thinking, his incredible energy and his unflinching confidence that he could overcome seemingly insurmountable odds. These traits that made his raids the subject of study for generations after him would also be the cause of his downfall.

The soldiers who followed Morgan into potential oblivion were also unique. They were tough, romantic, independent-thinking men who wanted something besides the rigors of Napoleonic military discipline. They wished to live on the edge. They hungered for adventure, danger and freedom. They harbored a particular distaste for camp life and army regulations. They wanted to make their enemy feel the real pain of war and do it on their own terms. They placed their full trust in John Hunt Morgan to accomplish their mission, so much so that they forever identified themselves as "Morgan's Men."

The officers and men who would bring Morgan to bay were unique, too. They had been embarrassed too many times by the likes of Morgan and his unorthodox approach to waging war. They were determined to stop the "guerrilla chief" and the "King of Horse Thieves" once and for all. Their extraordinary persistence, self-motivation and sheer willpower would do just that.

Morgan's Great Raid showcased the best and the worst of the soldiers of both sides. Like many occasions in war, the raid was beset with some of the worst acts of mankind: fratricide, theft and murder. Yet it also exhibited courage, determination, resilience and, yes, even compassion and love; these are among the best traits that humans can offer in times of great sorrow, death and destruction. In short, the Indiana-Ohio Raid is a microcosm of the American Civil War.

This book looks at Morgan's Great Raid of July 1863 with the intent of providing an overview of an extraordinary military operation. It does not go into great lyrical detail about the battles, soldiers and civilians as have some of the previous works written on the raid. Instead, this book tries to portray a general flavor for the event as it unfolded, the soldiers who made it happen and the civilian population affected by it. A unique aspect of this publication is the large set of detailed maps that depict the primary skirmishes and battles of the raid. Pictures can sometimes say a thousand words. These maps help show the complexity of Morgan's tactical thinking when he was engaged behind enemy lines. Within the space afforded in the pages that follow, it is hoped that the reader will gain a good understanding of why Morgan's Great Raid is important to American history.

I would like to acknowledge a few persons without whom this book would have never existed. Edd Sharp, the current president of the Ohio Civil War Trail Commission and the president of the Buffington Island Battlefield Preservation Foundation, was the person responsible for immersing me in the subject of Morgan's Ohio Raid over a dozen years ago. He offered me the opportunity to serve as a volunteer on the commission, and it has changed my life for the better. Furthermore, Edd's willpower and determination to complete the Ohio John Hunt Morgan Heritage Trail project have inspired me over these many years. Thank you, Edd, for all that you have done. I would also like to thank Lora Cahill, a talented researcher and author who encouraged me to take my research and put it into print. Everyone needs another to "push oneself into the pool," so to speak, or else one may never swim. Lora did that for me, and I am forever grateful. Finally, I would like to thank Hal Jespersen for his awesome talent and patience in taking my numerous hand-drawn maps and converting them into the works of art you will see in this book. In addition to offering his cartographic skills to authors, Hal volunteers his services to the online Civil War community. His talent has touched the lives of a whole new generation of history seekers. Keep it going, Hal!

Chapter 1

"Knight on a White Horse"

By early June 1863, when Confederate brigadier general John Hunt Morgan first proposed his daring raid into the North, most citizens of the South felt they were winning the American Civil War, even though the tide had already turned against them. For over a year, Union ground forces had been steadily infiltrating and occupying key portions of the fledgling country. They had captured New Orleans, Memphis and Nashville, three of the Confederacy's largest providers of war materiel. The Union navy's successful blockade of the Confederacy's major coastal ports prevented Southern trade for foreign goods, causing the Confederate economy to deteriorate faster. In the political war, President Abraham Lincoln's signing of the Emancipation Proclamation in January 1863 deterred any notion that Great Britain or France may have had to back the Confederacy and its abhorrent institution of slavery.

The Confederacy's best attempts to retake its lost territory and bring the war to the Northern states had failed miserably in the autumn of 1862. General Braxton Bragg's Army of Tennessee, the most powerful force defending the Confederate states west of the Appalachian Mountains, was turned back at the Battle of Perryville, Kentucky, in October. Bragg retreated ingloriously into Tennessee, never again to enter Kentucky with a force of conquering magnitude.

East of the mountains, General Robert E. Lee's Army of Northern Virginia was defeated in September at the gory Battle of Antietam (Sharpsburg) in Maryland. The Union Army of the Potomac held the field, while the Confederates slipped back into Virginia to fight another day. Nonetheless, Lee's losses at Antietam were so great that he knew another invasion of the North was out of the question, at least not until he could gather more equipment and men, which the Confederacy had few to provide. Thus, Lee placed his army into a defensive position in northern Virginia, awaiting the onslaught of the Federals' seemingly overwhelming manpower and limitless supplies.

Northern citizens perceived the battles at Perryville and Antietam to be "indecisive bloodbaths" rather than victories that had turned the tide of the Civil War in their favor. In both campaigns, the Confederate armies had escaped the fatal blows that the war-weary Northern people expected their commanders to deliver. To appease his angry constituency, Lincoln chose to relieve the commanders who had led the Union armies at Perryville and Antietam—Major General Don Carlos Buell and Major General George B. McClellan, respectively. In the late autumn of 1862, the North's willingness to continue the war effort hung in the balance. In the tip of this scale rested the South's last real hope to win the war.

Despite his defeat in the Kentucky Campaign, General Bragg remained confident that he could hold Middle and East Tennessee against the Federal juggernaut. Bragg believed Major General William Rosecrans's Union Army of the Cumberland would not move out of its Nashville fortifications until the springtime. Confederate president Jefferson Davis agreed, so much so that he transferred nearly one-sixth of the Army of Tennessee to Lieutenant General John C. Pemberton to bolster the defenses at Vicksburg, Mississippi, a city that both sides considered vital to winning the war. However, Bragg's and Davis's overly optimistic views of the situation in Middle Tennessee quickly dissolved around New Year's Day 1863, when Rosecrans's army engaged Bragg's in a violent three-day struggle among the snow-caked, blood-spattered cedars surrounding Murfreesboro (Stones River). Like Lee, Bragg reacted to this indecisive slaughter by choosing a defensive strategy that would allow him to refurbish his broken army with men and materiel. He retreated southward and formed a line along the headwaters of the Duck River north of Shelbyville and Manchester. Bragg licked his wounds there for the next six months, while Rosecrans, hovering around Murfreesboro, prepared his army for the final fatal thrust.

After the Battle of Stones River, President Abraham Lincoln and the Northern citizenry finally sensed the turn in the war effort. "I can never forget, whilst I remember anything," Lincoln wrote later to Rosecrans, "you

General Braxton Bragg permitted Morgan's raid into Kentucky but did not authorize its extension into Indiana and Ohio. Bragg later commanded the Confederate army at the Battles of Chickamauga and Chattanooga. He attempted to disband Morgan's raiders but was thwarted. *Courtesy of the Library of Congress.*

gave us a hard-earned victory, which, had there been a defeat instead, the nation could scarcely have lived over." The North began to believe that an attack on the hibernating Southern armies could perhaps destroy them, or at the least, it could take away more ground from the Confederacy.

One such offensive began in the early spring of 1863. Union major general Ulysses S. Grant's Army of the Tennessee made a bold move against Vicksburg, the last major Confederate bastion on the Mississippi River. If Vicksburg fell, the western Confederacy undoubtedly would be split in two, and the Union navy would have complete control of the Mississippi River, a critical avenue of military transport and a natural barrier for enemy ground troops. President Lincoln considered Vicksburg a top target for his western armies.

For the first two years of the war, it seemed General Pemberton's Army of Mississippi held an impregnable position at Vicksburg that no enemy could take. Grant and his right-hand man, Major General William Tecumseh Sherman, had made four unsuccessful attempts to capture the citadel during the winter of 1862–63 and into the following spring. Their first campaign in December 1862 had ended miserably in the swamps below Chickasaw Bluffs and in the woodlands north of Grenada, Mississippi, at a cost of over 1,700 Federal casualties. A canal construction project and two subsequent water-borne campaigns in the bayous north of Vicksburg also had floundered.

Undaunted by these successive failures, in April 1863, Grant launched a new campaign to capture Vicksburg from the Louisiana shore. Using the armada of Admiral David D. Porter's U.S. Navy fleet, Grant surprised Pemberton by executing a daring amphibious landing south of the city. Grant's army immediately followed its success with a brilliant flanking march through Jackson that bottled up the Confederates among the outskirts of Vicksburg. By June 1863, it appeared Grant had the upper hand on Pemberton, and it would only be a matter of time until Vicksburg would capitulate. Even worse, the Army of Mississippi would certainly be lost with it.

During the same time period, two Federal campaigns occurred east of the Appalachians, but they failed to achieve the same successes as those of Rosecrans and Grant. Major General Ambrose Burnside led the Army of the Potomac against Lee in Northern Virginia, but the Union campaign ended in disaster at the Battle of Fredericksburg in December 1862, and Burnside was relieved of command. The following April, Union major general Joseph Hooker led a refreshed Army of the Potomac across the Rappahannock River, initially catching Robert E. Lee by surprise. However, Lee countered this threat with a brilliant victory at the Battle of Chancellorsville, Virginia, during the first days of May. Hooker's army retreated northward in dismay, once again thwarted by the smaller Army of Northern Virginia. For his efforts, Lee attained the enduring status of a hero among the people of the South.

The victories at Fredericksburg and Chancellorsville, ones that the Confederate nation desperately needed to maintain its morale, also gave Lee the impetus he desired to plan another invasion of the North. Lee and Davis decided the Army of Northern Virginia was ready to take the offensive again. They understood that taking the war to the Union states might sway the Northern people's attitude toward a quick resolution of the war through recognition of the Confederacy as its own sovereign country. Lee planned to invade Maryland and Pennsylvania through the Shenandoah Valley and, if successful in defeating the Army of the Potomac, perhaps capture Harrisburg, Pennsylvania. He began his offensive, later known as the Gettysburg Campaign, in the middle part of June 1863.

The Confederacy west of the Appalachians still sought a hero like Lee. The nation needed a great victory in the West that would send the bluecoat invaders scurrying back into Kentucky and beyond. The nation searched for a leader who could deliver a knockout blow. Unfortunately, General Braxton Bragg would not prove to be the hero the Confederacy was searching for.

"Knight on a White Horse"

Throughout the first six months of 1863, General Bragg did little to change his war strategy or to fully understand Rosecrans's plans. Instead, Bragg used the time to reorganize his convalescing army with the thought of eliminating the subordinates he thought were to blame for the defeat at Murfreesboro. The reorganization affected all branches of his army; Bragg selected new leaders he felt he could trust. Unfortunately, he failed to comprehend how badly he had fragmented and demoralized the Army of Tennessee's command structure.

Bragg also realized that his Army of Tennessee's position along the Duck River was vulnerable. If Grant was to take Vicksburg and capture Pemberton's army, Grant could then turn his full attention toward Bragg's left flank. In addition, another threat loomed farther to the north. Major General Ambrose Burnside, the new commander of the Department of the Ohio, was piecing together a large army in Kentucky that would attack Bragg's lightly defended right flank under Major General Simon Bolivar Buckner at Cumberland Gap, Tennessee.

Ambrose Everett Burnside was born in 1824 near the hamlet of Liberty, Indiana, situated about forty miles northwest of Cincinnati. An 1847 graduate of West Point, he served in the Mexican-American War and on the American frontier until he resigned from the army in 1853. Returning to civilian life in Rhode Island, he invented the Burnside breech-loading rifle, started an unsuccessful company and worked in the railroad business. At the beginning of the Civil War, he organized the First Rhode Island Infantry and saw action at the First Battle of Manassas, where he earned a brigadier general's star. He gained national acclaim for his successful amphibious expedition on the North Carolina coast, for which he was promoted in March 1862.

As the leader of the IX Corps at Antietam, and later as commander of the Union Army of the Potomac, Burnside failed to make good impressions on the battlefield. President Lincoln relieved him from command of the Army of the Potomac after the disastrous Fredericksburg Campaign of December 1862. Burnside was reassigned on March 23, 1863, to head the Department of the Ohio, a military zone that encompassed the states of Ohio, Indiana, Illinois, Michigan, Wisconsin, West Virginia and the portion of Kentucky lying east of the Tennessee River. In this "desk job" position, Burnside reorganized the department's forces into the XXIII Corps, or Army of the Ohio. Burnside did very well in quelling the excessive Copperhead (Peace Democrat) activities in his department, and he prevented wholesale rioting from occurring in his region after the institution of the Federal draft.

From his headquarters building on Ninth Street between Vine and Walnut Streets in Cincinnati, Burnside planned to fulfill Lincoln's desire for an invasion of East Tennessee. If Grant and Burnside were to move simultaneously, they could outflank Bragg's army or, even worse, cut it off from its supply base at Chattanooga, Tennessee. If Bragg could not hold Rosecrans at Tullahoma, Bragg knew he would be forced to fall back toward Chattanooga. In a worst-case scenario, he would establish a new line of defense south of the Tennessee River. By doing so, he would give up Middle Tennessee to the enemy, a loss the Confederacy could ill afford.

Major General Ambrose E. Burnside coordinated all the Federal ground and naval forces that chased Morgan's raiders. He later commanded Union forces at the Siege of Knoxville and the Battle of the Crater. *Courtesy of the Library of Congress.*

In the ensured face-off with his foe, Bragg would rely heavily on his cavalry to screen his army and obtain intelligence about the enemy. He left the chore of accomplishing these tasks to Major General Joseph Wheeler, head of the Army of Tennessee's cavalry corps. Wheeler had won Bragg's trust as an obedient subordinate. Although unfit for independent command, Wheeler was a brave cavalry leader with a talent for protecting a large army. Hence, Wheeler served Bragg's needs. But Bragg's inability to make the best use of his officers' talents hamstrung Wheeler's more independent-minded subordinates, Brigadier General John Hunt Morgan and Brigadier General Nathan Bedford Forrest.

Morgan and Forrest understood that cavalry could be more effective when used for quick strikes on enemy supply lines rather than employed for only picketing and scouting. During the first two years of the Civil War, cavalry attacks of this kind had proven to cause disruptions to enemy campaigns. For example, General Grant's first campaign to capture Vicksburg was halted when Confederate major general Earl Van Dorn's cavalry raid destroyed Grant's base of supplies at Holly Springs, Mississippi, in December 1862. Grant learned from Van Dorn's success. He sent Union colonel Benjamin Grierson on an April 1863 cavalry raid from LaGrange, Tennessee, to Baton Rouge, Louisiana, to divert the attention of General Pemberton's Confederate forces away from Grant as his army approached Vicksburg. Grierson's Mississippi Raid not only achieved its objective but also went down in American history as one of the greatest raids of all time. Most of all, it proved the Union cavalry had risen to a level equal in strength and skill to the Confederate cavalry in the western theater of the war.

Braxton Bragg also recognized the power of the cavalry to divert the enemy's attention away from an army. He wanted a similar diversion as Grierson's to hold Rosecrans's and Burnside's attentions long enough for the Army of Tennessee to fall back safely to a better defensive position. "General Bragg," wrote Colonel Basil W. Duke of Morgan's command, "knew how to use, and invariably used, his cavalry to good purpose, and in this emergency he resolved to employ some of it to divert from his own hazardous movement, and fasten upon some other quarter, the attention of a portion of the opposing forces." A leader in Wheeler's corps offered a proposal. The officer's name was John Hunt Morgan.

The handsome, dashing thirty-eight-year-old brigadier general hailed from a prominent pro-Confederate family in Lexington, Kentucky. One Confederate soldier asked, "Did you ever see Morgan on horseback? If not, you missed one of the most impressive figures of the war. Perhaps no General in either army surpassed him in the striking proportion and grace of his person, and the ease and grace of his horsemanship." At six feet tall, 185 pounds, broad shouldered, with sparkling gray blue eyes and a well-trimmed black beard and mustache, he was a compelling man to behold.

John Hunt Morgan was born in 1825 in Huntsville, Alabama, to a family with Southern aristocratic ties to Kentucky millionaire John Wesley Hunt. Morgan grew up in the world of Southern high society and its definition of honor. He briefly attended Transylvania University in Lexington, Kentucky, but higher education did not suit him; he quit school in 1844 in search of a permanent commission in the United States Marine Corps. Although this opportunity never manifested itself, the advent of the Mexican-American War offered John the chance he needed to enter the military. In June 1846, Morgan volunteered as a private in Company K of Colonel Humphrey Marshall's First Regiment of Kentucky Mounted Volunteers and was subsequently promoted to first lieutenant. John saw action in the Battle of

A drawing of Brigadier General John Hunt Morgan at the time of his death in 1864. While traversing enemy territory, Morgan dressed in plain clothes to make it harder for snipers to distinguish him from his troopers. *Courtesy of the Library of Congress.*

Buena Vista in Mexico, where the regiment handled itself well. When the war ended, Morgan again searched for a way to make military service a lasting occupation. Meanwhile, he ran several lucrative businesses that made him wealthy and well respected in Lexington society. In 1857, John used his wealth to fund and train sixty men to form a militia company called the Lexington Rifles. This well-drilled military group became the toast of the city's Southern aristocracy.

However, John Morgan also harbored a darker side to his personality. He frequently suffered bouts of depression that would affect him for weeks at a time. To counteract his melancholic fits, he often gambled, drank heavily and enjoyed the company of loose women—all respectable acts in upper-class antebellum Southern society. Duke testified that Morgan never did anything that "touched his integrity as a man and his honor as a gentleman...The qualities in General Morgan, which would have attracted most attention in private life, were an exceeding gentleness of disposition and unbounded generosity. His kindness and goodness of heart were proverbial." After his wife became so severely ill that she required continual care, Morgan delayed joining his comrades in the Civil War by four months so that he could stay by his wife's side. In the end, John Morgan was a good husband and a caring, honorable citizen. He understood his own flaws, and he tolerated the faults of others—a characteristic found in good leadership.

Morgan had already earned accolades for his daring thrusts deep behind Union lines to disrupt enemy communications, reinforcements and supplies. His targets were things, not armies. Morgan was a colleague of the brilliant Confederate cavalry leader Nathan Bedford Forrest, who thought that horses should be used as a mode of transport for infantrymen. Unlike the standard cavalrymen who were armed with sabers and pistols, which were good only for hand-to-hand fighting, the infantrymen possessed rifles and artillery—firepower that could defeat opponents at long range. Forrest and Morgan shared the strategy that infantrymen mounted on horses were more maneuverable and thus more effective than the standard infantrymen who traveled on foot. Infantrymen mounted on horses had the necessary firepower, endurance and quickness to capture enemy outposts protecting railroads, steamboats and wagons—the key modes of transport for supplies and reinforcements. If the outposts could be disabled temporarily, then destruction of the enemy's support system could be accomplished. Such destruction would naturally hinder or completely stop the enemy in their ability to wage war at the front. This strategy is not unlike the modern-day tactics of the United States Special Operations Command, whose units include the army's Delta Force and the navy's SEALs.

Morgan put his strategy to the test by conducting several dangerous operations in Union-held territory, particularly in central and western Kentucky, where he and his "raiders" were familiar with the roads and the countryside. The stunning success of their raids at Bacon Creek Trestle, Kentucky, in December 1861; at Cave City, Kentucky, in May 1862; at Cynthiana, Kentucky, in July 1862; at Gallatin, Tennessee, in August 1862; at Lexington, Kentucky, in October 1862; and at Muldraugh's Hill, Kentucky, in late December 1862 had earned them the praise of the Confederate people and the ire of the Union high command.

Morgan's victory at the Battle of Hartsville, Tennessee, in early December 1862, was the greatest battlefield triumph of his career. Within days, President Jefferson Davis rewarded Morgan with a brigadier general's star and a division of cavalry. While Southern newspapers gave him the sobriquets the "Marion of the War" and "Thunderbolt of the Confederacy," Southern children recited this popular poem:

I wanted to be a cavalryman
And with John Hunt Morgan ride,
A Colt revolver in my belt
A sabre by my side.
I wanted a pair of epaulets
To match my suit of gray,
The uniform my mother made
And lettered C.S.A.

Morgan was the hero the western Confederacy desperately sought.

Inspired by Grierson's Mississippi Raid, Morgan came to his superiors, Wheeler and Bragg, in June 1863 with the thought that anything the Union cavalry could do, Morgan's Men could do better. Unlike the people of the South, Bragg was not personally fond of Morgan. After the war, he expressed his opinion of Morgan in a communication to former president Jefferson Davis. "General Morgan was an officer who had few superiors, none, perhaps, in his own line, but," claimed Bragg, "he was a *dangerous* man, on account of his intense desire to act independently."

Yet Morgan's proposal for a diversionary raid piqued Bragg's interest. As Bragg understood it, Morgan's plan was to take his cavalry division across the Cumberland River, which marked the approximate line of the Union army. From there, Morgan would drive his men deep into Kentucky and threaten Louisville, a major Union military depot for supplies and reinforcements. Along the way, he could perhaps recruit more Kentuckians to join the Confederate army, a motive that Bragg had used to invade Kentucky the previous year. Maybe Morgan was aware that Wheeler had suggested the same idea to Bragg on March 7, 1863. Wheeler believed that a cavalry raid on Louisville could be accomplished in fifteen days and could gain large quantities of valuable supplies for the Confederate army. Bragg had promised to authorize Wheeler's raid on Louisville when "satisfied the enemy [Rosecrans] will not advance" and "as soon as a force can be spared."

However, in Morgan's mind, a raid on Louisville was insufficient. What Morgan *intended* to do was to take his cavalrymen across the Ohio River, ride through Indiana and Ohio and then return to Confederate lines in southern Kentucky. By entering into the Northern states, Morgan believed that the Northern people would show such great anxiety over having a Confederate force on their soil that they would insist on the maximum protection of their military. The result would be that Rosecrans and Burnside would have no choice but to send large contingents of their armies to chase Morgan's Division across Indiana and Ohio rather than send them against Bragg.

Morgan kept his real intentions secret from Bragg and Wheeler. Morgan had already decided that the overly cautious Bragg would never approve a plan to cross the Ohio River. It was too risky. If Morgan took his division beyond Kentucky's borders, Bragg would not be able to recall these cavalrymen to protect the Army of Tennessee's flanks in case of emergency. Morgan perhaps thought that Bragg did not trust him enough to accomplish a mission of this magnitude, even though his track record with guerrilla warfare had been impeccable. Simply put, Morgan was convinced that Bragg would never accept the idea of a raid into the Northern states.

On the night of June 10, 1863, Morgan gathered together his officers and revealed to them his actual plan. They were going to enter the Bluegrass State and then cross the Ohio River near Louisville. From there they would sweep across Indiana and Ohio, destroying military targets and diverting enemy troops. If possible, they might link with General Lee's army in Pennsylvania or return to Confederate lines by way of Virginia. Morgan believed the four greatest obstacles for the raid would be 1) crossing the Cumberland River, 2) crossing the Ohio River, 3) circumventing Cincinnati—particularly the Cincinnati, Hamilton & Dayton Railroad—and 4) recrossing the Ohio River. To gather more intelligence about these obstacles, he had sent scouts under Captain Thomas Hines into Indiana and Ohio three weeks earlier to record the best places to cross the Ohio River and to map the safest roads around Cincinnati. One of those crossings was at Buffington Island, which sat on the river separating Ohio from West Virginia. As usual, Morgan seemed to have all his bases covered. The officers were in agreement with the plan, although not without serious apprehension.

What Morgan had failed to tell them was that by crossing the Ohio River, they would be in direct disobedience of General Bragg's orders to remain close enough to be quickly recalled to Tennessee. Morgan informed only one officer—Colonel Basil Duke, Morgan's second-in-command—of this fact. Duke did not bother to talk his commander out of executing an operation that he had wanted to do for more than a year. "General Morgan's ideas regarding the movement...were definite and fixed." Morgan was adamant that his raiders could not achieve their objective unless they touched on Northern soil. He refused to let Bragg's timidity spoil his plan. After all, Grierson's cavalrymen had been able to ride across Mississippi successfully; why couldn't Morgan's men do the same in Indiana and Ohio?

Morgan had recruited men from Kentucky who had grown up around fast horses and who were willing to share the risks involved with going behind enemy lines. Yet Morgan's fame stretched far beyond the Bluegrass State. From all across the country, young men, many only just boys, thronged to the general's ranks. Biographer James A. Ramage described Morgan's widespread attraction as "appealing to the romantic hope that a knight on a white horse could lead mounted men to victory. Morgan promised adventure, romance, and success, all of which were woefully missing in the regular service." Most of "Morgan's Men," as they came to proudly call themselves, were under the age of twenty-six. Their officers had proven themselves in battle and had showed the courage to lead these youths into a territory where every turn of the corner might reveal a Union cavalry patrol or defensive position. Most importantly, General Morgan was willing to take every precaution and make every decision necessary to accomplish his mission and to get his men back safely within Confederate lines. His soldiers understood that Morgan was equal to the task at hand and that he would not order them anywhere he was not willing to go himself. Historian Edward Longacre noted that "Morgan's troopers, whom many observers believed the most reckless in the Confederate service, would have followed their commander to Siberia had he hankered to take them there." An acute sense of loyalty developed among Morgan's Men; Morgan endeared himself to his soldiers, and they to him.

Bragg and Wheeler issued a series of orders authorizing Morgan's Raid. The first of these was an order from Wheeler dated June 14, 1863, in which Bragg gave his permission for Morgan to immediately take 1,500 men into Kentucky and to leave the rest of his division to screen Bragg's army in Middle Tennessee. Wheeler's order also explicitly stated, "Should you hear that the enemy is advancing for a general engagement, General Bragg wishes you to turn rapidly and fall upon his [Rosecrans's] rear." Morgan pleaded with Bragg and Wheeler that 1,500 men were inadequate for this venture:

> McMINNVILLE, *June 15, 1863.*
>
> *Maj. Gen. JOSEPH WHEELER:*
> *Your dispatch is just received. Can accomplish everything with 2,000 men and four guns. To make the attempt with less, might prove disastrous, as large details will be required at Louisville to destroy the transportation, shipping, and Government property. Can I go? The result is certain.*
>
> JOHN H. MORGAN,
> *Brigadier-General.*

In response, Bragg sent another order on June 18 authorizing Morgan to take 2,000 men with artillery support. In return for the additional men, Bragg expected Morgan to destroy enemy supply depots, bridges and track along the Louisville & Nashville Railroad, Rosecrans's lifeline to the North. Morgan interpreted this series of orders in his own way by leaving behind 280 men of Colonel W.C.P. Breckinridge's Ninth Kentucky Cavalry regiment to secure Bragg's flank. Morgan stole away with the rest of the division, which amounted to 2,460 effectives.

Most of Morgan's men armed themselves with medium-length or short-barreled Enfield rifles and a pair of Colt pistols. Only officers carried cavalry sabers because the saber was useless for the raiders' style of fighting. "The trooper that attempted to carry one would be forever after a laughing stock for the entire command," one raider wrote. If Enfields could not be acquired, the men carried shotguns, breech-loading carbines and various muskets from the pre–Civil War days.

Since the cavalry was the worst-equipped branch of the Confederate army, Morgan's men scavenged anything they could find. Confederate uniforms were in short supply for the cavalry; thus, Morgan's men often had to confiscate blue uniforms from Union cavalrymen or wear civilian clothes. The Confederate cavalrymen even had to provide their own horses. Morgan's men had no choice but to requisition horses from civilians if they could not be taken from enemy soldiers. "General Morgan took fresh horses," Duke explained, "to enable his command to make the tremendous marches which ensured so much of his success, and to prevent his men from falling into the hands of the enemy, but he hedged around the practice with limitations which somewhat protected the citizen." All these foraging actions were sanctioned by the Confederate high command. Besides, by 1863, it was common practice among Union cavalrymen to take food and horses from civilians. It was war, after all.

Attached to the division was Captain Edward P. Byrne's four-gun battery of artillery. The four cannons were the types often found to support infantry as well as cavalry. The battery contained two twelve-pounder field howitzers, which Bragg's ordnance officer had just recently assigned to the division. Unfortunately, these heavier, less mobile newcomers had replaced the beloved "Bull Pup" mountain howitzers that had earned the admiration of Morgan's soldiers since the summer of 1862. "It came near raising a mutiny in the [Second Kentucky Cavalry] regiment," recalled Duke. In addition to the new howitzers, there were two three-inch Parrott rifles that Morgan's men had captured from Captain Benjamin S. Nicklin's Thirteenth Indiana

An 1863 photograph showing some of Morgan's raiders eating while prisoners of war in the Western Penitentiary, Pennsylvania. Lieutenant Leeland Hathaway, Fourteenth Kentucky Cavalry, sits at center. They were all captured during the Great Raid. Note their varying garb, typical of Morgan's men. *Courtesy of Hunt-Morgan House Deposit, University of Kentucky.*

Battery at the Battle of Hartsville. One of the Parrotts had an unusually long barrel that earned it the nickname "Long Tom." Because the Parrotts possessed exceptional range and accuracy, they were often detached on special duty under the command of Lieutenant Elias D. Lawrence. The Parrott rifle had the ability to consistently hit a target from a mile away. Artillery of this nature provided Morgan the firepower he needed to reduce a Union blockhouse or a small fort.

Morgan's successful raids had made recruiting for his division much easier than for many other Confederate units in late 1862 and early 1863. Young men eager for adventure and life on the edge had flocked to Morgan's camp to join his now-famous cavalry unit. By the beginning of the summer of 1863, Morgan's Division contained men from nearly every Confederate state. They were organized as follows:

MORGAN'S CAVALRY DIVISION Brig. Gen. John Hunt Morgan	
First Brigade Col. Basil W. Duke	**Second Brigade** Col. Adam R. Johnson
2nd Kentucky Cavalry, Maj. Thomas B. Webber	7th Kentucky Cavalry, Lt. Col. John M. Huffman
5th Kentucky Cavalry, Col. D. Howard Smith	8th Kentucky Cavalry, Col. Roy S. Cluke
6th Kentucky Cavalry, Col. J. Warren Grigsby	10th Kentucky Cavalry, Maj. George W. Owen
9th Tennessee Cavalry, Col. William W. Ward	11th Kentucky Cavalry, Col. David W. Chenault (Lt. Col. Joseph T. Tucker, beginning July 4, 1863)
9th Kentucky Cavalry (Co. A), Capt. Thomas H. Hines	14th Kentucky Cavalry, Col. Richard C. Morgan
Kentucky Battery (two 3-inch Parrott rifles; two 12-pounder howitzers) Capt. Edward P. Byrne	

General John Hunt Morgan's two brigade commanders were seasoned leaders of guerrilla-style warfare. Many considered Morgan's brother-in-law and First Brigade commander, Colonel Basil Duke, the "brains" of the division. Duke had shown early on that he possessed a special ability for strategic planning and logistics. Morgan placed his full trust in Duke when it came to military and personal matters.

Twenty-six-year-old Basil Wilson Duke was born an only child to a Southern aristocratic, slaveholding family in Lexington, Kentucky. He attended Transylvania University and moved to St. Louis, Missouri, where he practiced law. He was more into politics than law, and when the Federal government threatened the Southern aristocracy's way of life, Duke became a staunch secessionist. When the Civil War broke out, he joined the Missouri State Militia, and after a brief leave of absence in Kentucky to marry Henrietta "Tommie" Morgan (John Hunt Morgan's younger sister), Duke returned to Missouri to fight with the Confederate army under General William Hardee, whom Duke served as an adjutant and a scout. His service

As second-in-command, Colonel Basil W. Duke led a brigade in Morgan's Division. He was promoted to lead the division after Morgan's death. Duke became a powerful Lost Cause advocate and a prolific writer after the war. Theodore Roosevelt was a close friend. *Courtesy of Hunt-Morgan House Deposit, University of Kentucky.*

as a scout taught him much about the effectiveness of hit-and-run techniques. He often worked closely with future guerrilla leaders John S. Marmaduke and Jeff Thompson. However, it was Hardee who spotted Duke's talent as a cavalryman; Hardee recommended to Duke that he return to Kentucky to recruit a cavalry regiment there. Duke accepted the advice.

By pure coincidence, Duke came in contact with Captain John Hunt Morgan and his Lexington Rifles at Munfordville, Kentucky, in September 1861. Duke was happy that his brother-in-law led a cavalry unit. Duke joined the seventy-five-man Lexington Rifles as a private, but the men elected him to first lieutenant and second-in-command of the unit. It is believed Duke convinced Morgan to use the Rifles in the same capacity that Duke had used his scouts in Missouri. Morgan must have agreed. Since Morgan was not interested in the mundane routines of military training and administration, he left these tasks to Duke. Duke was a natural in this role. The men adored his wit and charm, and he seemed to understand their needs. More than anything, he was brave in the face of the enemy and commanded respect.

Using his knowledge gained in Missouri, Duke effectively trained the Lexington Rifles in the art of hit-and-run raids. On October 27, 1861, Morgan, Duke and the "Old Squadron," as they would forever call themselves, mustered into the Confederate service as Company A, Second Kentucky Cavalry—the core around which Morgan's Division would develop. With Duke serving as an organizer and tactician, and Morgan brandishing his audacity and leadership, their partnership would create one of America's most innovative and effective independent cavalry units.

Duke understood far too well the dangers of going deep into enemy territory, but it did not deter his lust for action. In September 1862, Duke attempted to cross the Ohio River on a raid of his own design, but it ended in disaster at the Battle of Augusta, Kentucky, where enemy home guards ambushed his force. Nonetheless, Duke was anxious to redeem himself and attempt another raid into Ohio, especially with Morgan at the helm.

Morgan's Second Brigade commander, Colonel Adam "Stovepipe" Johnson, had also earned a great reputation as a guerrilla-style fighter. Johnson revealed his unique adeptness toward guerrilla tactics through his raids on Union outposts in western Kentucky and western Tennessee.

Twenty-nine-year-old Adam Rankin Johnson was born and raised in Henderson, a town located in the heart of western Kentucky. In 1854, he moved to Burnet County on the Texas frontier, where he worked as a surveyor and as a supplier for Butterfield Overland Mail stations. He became an adept Indian fighter and was well known for his fearlessness and leadership in skirmishes with the Comanches. "Out of frontier necessity, he became an expert in combat misdirection and illusion," author Raymond Mulesky noted. In 1861, Johnson moved back to the state of his childhood to join a Confederate contingent under Lieutenant Colonel Nathan Bedford Forrest. Johnson's combat experience in Texas made him a perfect candidate to be a scout. In fact, Forrest considered him one of his best trackers. In May 1862, Johnson was given permission to recruit his own regiment called the Tenth Kentucky Partisan Rangers, better known as the Tenth Kentucky Cavalry. As colonel of this undersized unit, he demonstrated his unique guerrilla tactics through his quick-strike raids on Union outposts in western Kentucky. Though outnumbered by the enemy during most of his operations, the "Kentucky Swamp Fox" disrupted Union supply lines and created general havoc for Federal commanders.

In July 1862, during one of Adam Johnson's independent operations, Johnson put fewer than forty men across the Ohio River to attack the Federal supply depot at Newburgh, Indiana. The swift crossing caught the Indiana home guard completely by surprise. Johnson received his soubriquet "Stovepipe" by using stovepipes mounted on wagon wheels to trick the Union garrison into thinking that he possessed artillery. The bluecoat defenders, out of fear of being blasted to kingdom come, surrendered the town without a shot being fired. The daylong Newburgh Raid was a complete success, resulting in the first capture of a Northern town during the war and creating much panic among Federal authorities. General Morgan may have studied Johnson's Newburgh Raid during the planning stage for his Indiana-Ohio Raid. Having Colonel Johnson accompany him on his Indiana-Ohio Raid made Morgan

Colonel Adam R. "Stovepipe" Johnson commanded a brigade in Morgan's Division. Johnson escaped Ohio and temporarily led the remnants of the division until Morgan's return. Blinded in a skirmish in 1864, Johnson later founded Marble Falls, Texas, and wrote an autobiography. *Courtesy of U.S. Army HEC, MOLLUS Collection.*

even more confident that he could perform his own operation within the Northern states.

On June 11, from his base at Alexandria, Tennessee, General Morgan led his division north toward Carthage, Tennessee, in anticipation of the start of his raid. However, within a week, Morgan received a dispatch from General Bragg ordering him to delay his raid for the moment. Word had arrived at the Army of Tennessee's headquarters that Union colonel William P. Sanders was driving his cavalry brigade toward East Tennessee to possibly threaten Bragg's right flank around Knoxville and Cumberland Gap. Bragg needed Morgan to turn east and head off Sanders.

Reluctantly, Morgan moved his men eastward through a rugged, rain-soaked landscape. In doing so, his division used up precious time, energy and supplies that he had gathered specifically for their raid into the North. In the last week of June, when his division reached Albany, Kentucky, he received reports that Sanders's raiders had returned to Union lines in Kentucky. Morgan was frustrated; much had been lost for nothing gained.

Around June 23, following confirmation of Sanders's departure from East Tennessee, Morgan marched his division to the south bank of the Cumberland River near Burkesville, Kentucky. There the raiders waited yet another week to replenish their supplies. Morgan would not leave anything to chance during preparation time. He and his men knew that once they crossed the Cumberland, they were on their own. No one would be able to help them. They also knew Burnside's forces instantly would be hot on their tail, bent on sending them to prison or to an early grave.

Chapter 2

Thunderbolt on the Bluegrass

A t last, the moment arrived to launch the Indiana-Ohio Raid, also to be known as the Great Raid or the Ohio Raid. In the early evening of June 30, 1863, Colonel Dick Morgan's scouting regiment, the Fourteenth Kentucky Cavalry, rode toward Burkesville and began crossing the Cumberland River at Neely's Ferry and Oliver's Landing. The scouts would set up a defensive perimeter for the rest of the division. On the morning of July 1, Johnson's Second Brigade of about 1,000 men started crossing the river at the ferries several miles west of Burkesville, primarily McMillan's Ferry and Cloyd's Ferry. That evening, Duke's First Brigade of approximately 1,500 men moved into position along the south bank of the Cumberland River at the ferries south and east of Burkesville. The principal crossings Duke's men would use were Neely's Ferry, Burkesville Ferry, Scott's Ferry, Bakerton Ferry and Winfrey's Ferry.

The river ran above flood stage and was over a half mile wide, its swirling waters filled with debris and mud. A scattering of Union cavalry outposts guarded the river, but the defenders were under strength and unaware of the Confederates' presence. Although Burnside and Rosecrans had suspected that soon Morgan would be conducting another raid into Kentucky, they never thought anyone, even Morgan, would attempt to cross the river when it was flooded.

Morgan's raiders searched for canoes, boats and rafts. They lashed together the few they could find and placed boards across them. Upon these contraptions they loaded their artillery, wagons and equipment and ferried

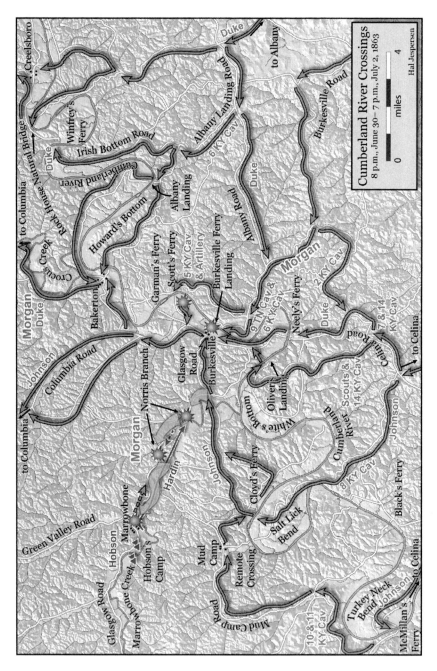

Map showing Morgan's crossings of the Cumberland River around Burkesville, Kentucky.
Author's collection.

Union colonel Frank L. Wolford led a brigade that included his crack fighting unit, the First Kentucky (U.S.) Cavalry. President Lincoln had Wolford arrested and discharged for his vocal opposition to the government. He became a leader of the Confederate amnesty movement in Kentucky. *Courtesy of the Library of Congress.*

them over on multiple trips throughout the night. Then the soldiers, some naked, swam the murky waters with their horses. Upon reaching the north bank, the wet men grabbed their guns and charged the few pickets of the First Kentucky (U.S.) Cavalry who had fired at them during the crossing. Outnumbered and surprised, the Union soldiers fled.

Union colonel Frank Wolford guarded the Burkesville sector at the time of Morgan's crossing. Forty-seven-year-old Frank Lane Wolford "was low of stature, but powerfully built, with storage room for lungs of immense capacity and bulk. His face was smooth-shaven and his hair iron-gray. His eye was, possibly, a more prominent feature than his nose; it fairly glowed with perceptible fire, was as keen as a hawk's, and like that of Marcus the Great, 'was able to pierce a corslet,' or 'gaze an eagle blind.'"

Despite coming from a poor family in Liberty, Kentucky, Wolford taught himself to be a lawyer. At the start of the Mexican-American War, he enlisted as a private in the Second Kentucky Infantry, whose muster rolls included George Rue and Edward Hobson. During his service in Mexico, Wolford made friends with John Hunt Morgan. Wolford distinguished himself at the Battle of Buena Vista when, exposed to a withering fire, he carried off the body of his commander, Lieutenant Colonel Henry Clay. After the war, Wolford was elected twice to the state House of Representatives, marking the beginning of a distinguished career in politics. Wolford became popular for his powerful oratories in and out of the courtroom. His stump speeches were printed throughout the nation.

Wolford raised the First Kentucky (U.S.) Cavalry in July 1861 and was commissioned its colonel. The regiment earned a reputation as a crack unit by friends and foes alike. "My boys know how to ride, how to shoot, how to fight and how to stand fire," Wolford claimed. "You may take any two Yankee regiments in the whole army—them two Michigan regiments over thar [*sic*] will do—station them where you please, on any ground, in town or country, in field or in forest, and I will take my regiment and what I don't kill of them I will chase out of the State of Tennessee in forty-eight hours." Wolford led his regiment in many engagements against his friend, John Hunt Morgan. In one such fight at Lebanon, Tennessee, on May 5, 1862, Morgan's men wounded and captured Wolford. Morgan personally offered Wolford a parole and safe passage, but Wolford refused. He was later freed. "Old Meat Axe" Wolford continued to impede Morgan, and they and their men became archrivals. The combat between Morgan's Division and Wolford's Cavalry matched Kentuckian against Kentuckian and brother against brother.

One Union commander who was not surprised by Morgan's maneuver on the Cumberland was Brigadier General Edward Henry Hobson. He would celebrate his thirty-eighth birthday during the upcoming campaign. "Gen. Hobson was a gallant officer, brave, but not rash; cool and determined in the midst of danger, and always at his post when there was work to do," noted one observer. "He was well liked by his men, and very popular in the army." He was born in Greensburg, Kentucky, and went to college in the neighboring town of Danville. He enlisted as a private in Company A, Second Kentucky Infantry, at the start of the Mexican-American War and rose to first lieutenant. After the war, Hobson became a successful businessman and banker. During the Civil War, he raised the Thirteenth Kentucky (U.S.) Infantry and led it gallantly at the Battle of Shiloh, which earned him a promotion to brigadier general. Assigned to guard the Green River line around Munfordville in November 1862, he had several run-ins with John Morgan. On one such occasion, Morgan tried to capture Hobson while he was on furlough at his Greensburg home, but Hobson successfully hid himself on a river cliff for over fourteen hours. At the time Morgan launched his Great Raid, Hobson commanded the Second Brigade in Brigadier General Henry Judah's Third Division, XXIII Corps.

Henry Moses Judah was a graduate of the West Point Class of 1843, the same group that claimed Ulysses S. Grant as a student. Judah excelled as a soldier in the Mexican-American War, earning praise for his bravery and rising to the rank of captain by the end of the conflict. During his postwar service in the Pacific Northwest, his colleagues found him drunk on duty, but before they could prefer charges against him, Judah transferred to the post at Placerville, California. At the outbreak of the Civil War, he served as the

Union brigadier general Edward H. Hobson led the pursuit of Morgan from Lebanon, Kentucky, to Buffington Island, Ohio. Ironically, Morgan captured Hobson at the 1864 Battle of Keller's Bridge, Kentucky. *Courtesy of the Guide to the Waveland State Shrine Photographic Collection, Special Collections, University of Kentucky.*

colonel of the Fourth California Infantry at Fort Yuma for several months before he resigned in November 1861 to go east. He performed duty in the defenses of Washington, D.C., until March 1862, when he was promoted to brigadier general. He served as inspector general to General Grant at Shiloh, but soon thereafter Major General Henry Halleck arranged for Judah to lead an infantry division, which performed well in the capture of Corinth, Mississippi. Judah was assigned to the inspector generalship of the Army of the Ohio in the winter of 1862–63, and the following spring, General Ambrose Burnside granted him command of the Third Division.

On June 30, only hours before Morgan began crossing the Cumberland, Hobson met with Judah to brief him on the situation in his sector. Hobson indicated that his scouts had found Colonel Adam Johnson's brigade camped in large numbers at Turkey Neck Bend. From this fact alone, Hobson believed Morgan was preparing to cross the river at any moment. To prevent

Brigadier General Henry M. Judah commanded the Union troops in the region where Morgan successfully penetrated the Cumberland River defensive line. Judah's poor decision-making during Morgan's Great Raid marked the beginning of the end of his career in the field. *Courtesy of the Library of Congress.*

this, Hobson proposed to attack Johnson at night and then post a brigade of Federal cavalry at Burkesville. Judah rejected both proposals. Instead, he ordered Hobson to Marrowbone, where he would defend the roads south of town. Judah would send Brigadier General James Shackelford's brigade from Glasgow to support Hobson.

Incredulous, Hobson called upon Colonel Richard T. Jacob and his Ninth Kentucky (U.S.) Cavalry to scout the area around Burkesville. "On the second day of July, I was ordered by General Hobson to send two hundred men, under a competent officer, if possible, to go into Burksville [*sic*]," remembered Jacob. "I sent Captain Hardin, an officer I had every confidence in."

About 11:00 a.m., Morgan's scouts reported Union cavalry advancing on the Glasgow Road from the direction of Marrowbone. The enemy's scouts were sighted four miles from Burkesville. Lieutenant Colonel Robert A.

Alston, Morgan's chief of staff, indicated that "it was supposed to be only a scouting party, and a portion of Dick Morgan's command was sent out to make a reconnaissance." Understanding the potential seriousness of the situation, General Morgan gathered up the nearest units he could find on the Burkesville side of the river. At about 1:00 p.m., he dashed off toward Marrowbone with 940 men consisting of Grigsby's Sixth Kentucky Cavalry, detachments from Ward's Ninth Tennessee Cavalry and Dick Morgan's Fourteenth Kentucky Cavalry, five companies of Huffman's Seventh Kentucky Cavalry and two pieces of Byrne's Battery.

Four miles from Burkesville, Morgan came upon a wide field bisected by a small creek named Norris Branch. He noticed that the enemy column marching southeast along the Marrowbone–Glasgow Road would be forced to ride around the western base of a high hill before reaching the Norris Branch cove. It seemed a good place for an ambush. The hill would hide Morgan's troopers until it was too late for the enemy to see them. Morgan deployed the Sixth Kentucky, Seventh Kentucky and artillery behind a brick house lying on the east side of the hill, while the detachments from the Ninth Tennessee and Fourteenth Kentucky lured the enemy down the Marrowbone Road in front of the house. As Morgan's scouts and the Ninth Tennessee fell back toward Norris Branch, Captain Thomas J. Hardin and his Union cavalrymen galloped after them. Hardin failed to detect the other Confederate cavalrymen and their artillery waiting in the cove behind the house. Holding their fire until the head of the Federal column entered the cove, Morgan's troopers and artillery suddenly let loose a volley that ripped into the Ninth Kentucky's left flank, causing the regiment to recoil. As the bewildered bluecoats reared their frightened horses in the direction of Marrowbone, the Fourteenth Kentucky and Ninth Tennessee fired into them, turning the Federal retreat into a rout. Morgan shouted for his men to charge the fleeing enemy, and the chase was on.

A running hand-to-hand fight ensued along a two-mile stretch of the Marrowbone–Glasgow Road. Lieutenant Kelion Franklin Peddicord of Company B, Fourteenth Kentucky Cavalry, observed something refreshing about his commander that he had not seen in many months. General Morgan, mounted on his horse, Glencoe, cheered his boys forward with his hat in hand and a familiar gleam in his eye. It was an inspiriting sight!

Captain Hardin rallied his troopers on a ridge overlooking the intersection of the Glasgow Road with the Dutch Creek Road. He dismounted his men along the crest on either side of the Glasgow Road. In a few minutes, Morgan's column came up and deployed into line of battle. "Our General,

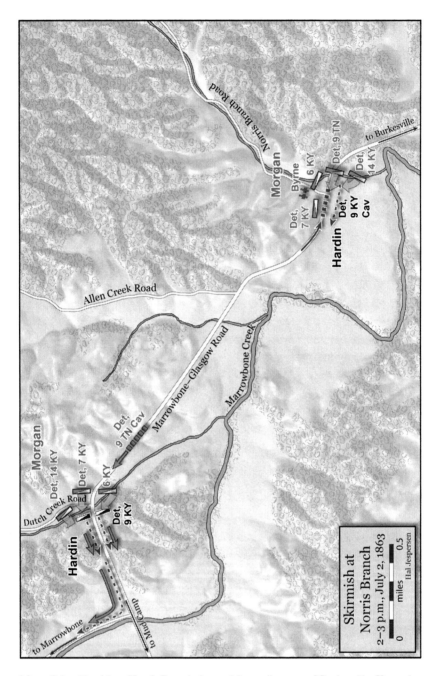

Map of the skirmish at Norris Branch, located four miles west of Burkesville, Kentucky. *Author's collection.*

who seemed more like our gallant Captain of old than he had for some time, was too shrewd for them," Peddicord wrote. "Quickly detaching a single scout around to their [enemy's] left flank secretly, with orders to fire his gun [rifle] and navies [revolvers] in rapid succession into their line, proved, much to our amusement, to have the desired effect. Back they flew again, using their rowels as vigorously as before."

For the next three miles, Morgan "drove the enemy back in confusion and at full speed, never letting them halt until they reached the encampment at Marrowbone." By 3:00 p.m., couriers brought Hobson news of Morgan's vigorous attack. Having previously been informed that his Twelfth Kentucky (U.S.) Cavalry was fending off Confederate cavalry from Johnson's brigade, Hobson assumed Marrowbone was about to be attacked by large numbers of the enemy. He immediately formed his infantry and artillery into line of battle behind Jacob's detachment of the Ninth Kentucky (U.S.) Cavalry. "Men sprang to their arms, and in an instant, some never stopping to put on their coats, haversacks, or canteens," wrote Captain Joseph P. Glezen of Company H, Eightieth Indiana Infantry. The men nervously watched as the dust cloud raised by Hardin's retreating cavalrymen drew toward them.

About 3:30 p.m., Hardin's exhausted cavalrymen filed rapidly into position alongside Jacob's ninety men. Their trailing cloud of dust obscured Morgan's view of Hobson's artillery and three infantry regiments supporting them. Suddenly, Morgan found himself galloping headlong toward hundreds of muskets aimed at him. One of the raiders grabbed Glencoe's reins and stopped the general just short of the Union line bristling with bayonets. "All saw it," recalled Peddicord, "and quickly wheeling our horses, with spurs in flanks, went out in true Indian style, lying flat on our horses, perhaps a little under." Seconds later, Jacob's cavalrymen opened fire at short range, and the Twenty-fourth Indiana Battery's six James six-pounders lobbed shells filled with grapeshot into the raiders' retreating column. Amazingly, only a handful of Morgan's men were hit.

The Union cavalry suffered five killed, fifteen wounded and fifteen captured, while the Confederates lost two mortally wounded and two slightly wounded. Colonel Jacob claimed three of his men captured on the road between Norris Branch and Marrowbone were shot down in cold blood by Morgan's men. Two of the prisoners died, but one lived to tell the story. Vengeance brewed in the minds of many of the Ninth Kentucky cavalrymen. Among the Confederate wounded was Captain Tom Quirk, the famed leader of Morgan's scouts, who had been hit twice—once in the hand

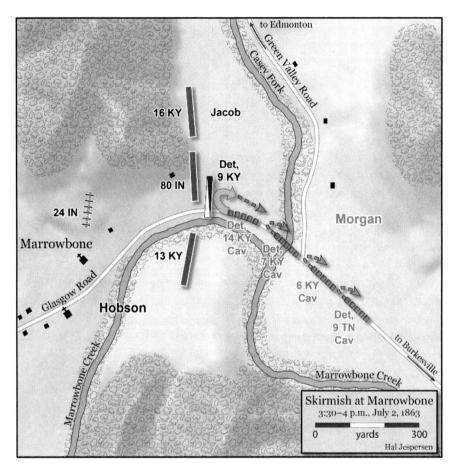

Map of the skirmish at Marrowbone, Kentucky. *Author's collection.*

and once in the rein arm—during the final charge at Marrowbone. Quirk would survive his wounds, but they would prevent him from continuing any farther on this raid. Morgan would have to make do without his experienced "eyes and ears."

By the late afternoon of July 2, Morgan's Division had completed its crossing of the Cumberland, thus marking the official start of the Great Raid. Morgan had removed the first major obstacle of the raid with little loss on his side. As the raiders marched north to Columbia, they saluted the masterminds of their success with their own marching song sporting the refrain "Here's the health to Duke and Morgan—Drink it down!" The men were thrilled to return to the Bluegrass State again.

Within hours, the alarm sounded at Rosecrans's and Burnside's headquarters that Morgan had forced a crossing at Burkesville. Both Union generals immediately sent urgent telegrams to Secretary of War Edwin M. Stanton in Washington. All realized the severe situation at hand. Rosecrans, already engaged in the first week of his great Tullahoma Campaign against Bragg, could not afford to send any of his troops to chase Morgan. Besides, it was within Burnside's territory that Morgan traveled.

On July 3, Burnside tried to set all his nearby units into motion. The Union commanders and soldiers in this part of Kentucky were well acquainted with Morgan's tactics. Most of them had tangled with Morgan's raiders at some time or another over the past two years of war. Speed was of the essence when confronting Morgan's troopers, but in the first days of the Indiana-Ohio Raid, it seemed that Union leadership had forgotten that fact.

Burnside's subordinate in control of operations in Kentucky was Brigadier General Jeremiah T. Boyle. Boyle's popularity in Kentucky was nonexistent. His overly harsh treatment of Kentucky's civilians made him perhaps the most hated man in the state. As commander of the District of Kentucky, a subdivision of the Department of the Ohio, Boyle owned the ultimate responsibility of dealing with Morgan while the Confederate raider moved within the state. However, Boyle was not a hands-on type of person. His style of leadership was more the "pass-the-buck" type. When Burnside gave Boyle orders, he simply passed them on to his subordinates without much thought. When Boyle's subordinates telegraphed him for assistance, Boyle would forward the telegrams to Burnside. For the most part, Boyle stayed in the middle of the Union communications throughout the raid, but he participated very little in the real effort to stop Morgan.

Boyle left that job to his field commanders in the region—Brigadier Generals Henry Judah, Edward Hobson and James Shackelford and Colonel Frank Wolford. Judah, the superior officer of the other three, was slow to respond to Burnside's orders to go after Morgan. Even when Hobson tried to send his cavalry to Burkesville on the morning of July 3, Judah countermanded the order. Judah's mishandling of his troops in the Burkesville-Columbia area had opened a large hole in the Union defense, allowing Morgan's Division to slip through mostly unmolested. Excuses from Judah ran rampant. As a result of his blunder, the subordinate Union commanders worked without coordination for another two days before Burnside took action to rectify the fiasco.

About noon on July 3, Morgan's scouts ran into a Union patrol consisting of men from their arch nemesis, the First Kentucky (U.S.) Cavalry. The Federal

Union brigadier general Jeremiah T. Boyle headed the District of Kentucky during Morgan's Great Raid. Boyle's passive leadership contributed to Morgan's quick penetration of the Cumberland River line and his successful crossing of the Ohio River. *Courtesy of U.S. Army HEC, MOLLUS Collection.*

cavalrymen had the upper hand in the beginning, but the advance guard slowly pushed back their Union counterparts to the southern outskirts of Columbia. Over an hour had elapsed before Colonel Richard Morgan, John's brother and the commander of the Fourteenth Kentucky Cavalry, formed his regiment in an apple orchard a half mile from town. Colonel Morgan sent for reinforcements; the Seventh and Second Kentucky Cavalry regiments responded, together with a section of Byrne's Battery. They dismounted into a line of battle on the ridge southwest of town.

Awaiting them were Union captain Jesse M. Carter and 150 men detached from three regiments of Colonel Frank Wolford's brigade. Carter was a seasoned officer of the First Kentucky (U.S.) Cavalry, "a man of Spartan bravery," and well acquainted with Morgan's raiders. During the initial fighting, Captain Carter, sitting tall on his horse, was mortally wounded while leading his dismounted troopers up the Burkesville–Glasgow Road past the Timoleon Cravens house. Carter managed to stay on his horse and ride back to a hotel on the square; he fell into a bed and died there later that night. Carter's First Kentucky detachment retreated to a fence behind the Cravens house and formed into line. When Carter fell mortally wounded, the command of the detachment devolved upon Captain John B. Fishback.

To meet the Confederate assault, the Forty-fifth Ohio Mounted Infantry dismounted and formed into a hollow square in a pasture between the M&F School and the Cravens house. Private Thomas Franklin Berry of Company B, Fourteenth Kentucky, called the Forty-fifth Ohio a "finely drilled body of men." He remembered how Byrne's "artillery poured grape and canister into their ranks just before our charging column

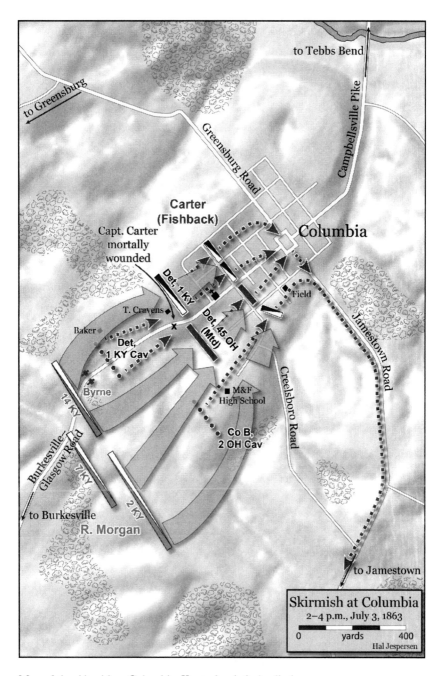

Map of the skirmish at Columbia, Kentucky. *Author's collection.*

reached them. Our headlong, swinging impact was more than they could stand. They were broken and their ranks thinned by the close range volleys of the charging squadrons." With a Rebel yell, Webber's Second Kentucky Cavalry charged the greatly outnumbered Company B, Second Ohio Cavalry, which withdrew into town with Fishback's other regiments. Fishback skillfully conducted a house-to-house defense of the town. Shooting out of windows and from behind houses, outbuildings and fence corners, the Union cavalrymen held back the Confederate attack long enough for the majority of Fishback's troops to escape down the Jamestown Road.

The two-hour skirmish at Columbia cost the Confederates four killed and seven wounded and the Federals four killed, eight wounded and several captured. Among the Confederate wounded was Captain Jacob T. Cassell, who the previous day had filled Tom Quirk's vacancy as commander of Morgan's scouts. Colonel Richard Morgan moved Captain Tom Franks of the Second Kentucky Cavalry into this seemingly cursed role.

Columbia's public square became the site of a victory celebration, the raiders guzzling whiskey taken from a local store. Morgan ordered the looting to cease. Lieutenant Colonel Alston fumed over his men's pilfering of the town after the fight: "Our men behaved badly at Columbia, breaking open a store and plundering it. I ordered the men to return the goods, and made all the reparation in my power. These outrages are very disgraceful, and are usually perpetrated by men accompanying the army simply for plunder. They are not worth a ———, and are a disgrace to both armies." Little did he know that this activity would worsen as the raid progressed. General Morgan's characteristic lack of enforcing discipline among his troops would stain his reputation for the rest of his life.

The Confederate rear guard did not clear the town until three hours after midnight. It encamped for the night in Cane Valley. Meanwhile, Duke ordered Captain Franks to scout the enemy at the Green River Bridge of the Columbia–Campbellsville Turnpike. Franks had been in his new job for only a few hours; little did he know that this night's scouting assignment would be one of the most important of the raid.

At dawn on July 4, Private Thomas Berry and many of his comrades heard some ominous news from Captain Franks's men. "Our scouts reported that during the entire night they heard the crashing of falling trees, and the sound of axes," wrote Berry. "We were destined to learn what this meant." The sounds had come from Union soldiers working nonstop through the night to cut down trees to block roads and clear a field of fire.

Defending the approaches to the bridge at the time of Morgan's Indiana-Ohio Raid were 266 men consisting of five companies of Colonel Orlando Hurley Moore's Twenty-fifth Michigan Infantry and a company-sized contingent from the Eighth Michigan and Seventy-ninth New York infantry regiments. Colonel Moore was experienced and fearless in battle, perhaps reckless at times. Before the war, as a lieutenant in the Sixth U.S. Infantry, he campaigned against the Cheyenne Indians. He was highly intellectual and was an accomplished violinist. The Twenty-fifth Michigan had spent most of its service defending the Louisville & Nashville Railroad against Confederate raids. Although the Michiganders had not been engaged in a major battle, Colonel Moore had seen to it that they were well trained and disciplined. They had become quite good marksmen with their Enfield rifles.

By June 30, Moore knew Morgan's raiders threatened to enter the region again. Although his force was greatly outnumbered, he decided to make a stand at the bridge rather than abandon it freely. Accordingly, Colonel Moore took full advantage of the strong defensive opportunities that the rugged terrain at Tebbs Bend offered. Moore's soldiers dug a semicircular fortification and a forward rifle pit across a one-hundred-yard narrows where the Columbia–Campbellsville Turnpike followed the top of a high razorback ridge bounded on two sides by the steep forested bluffs of the Green River. Vertically placed logs with sharpened points and hacked-out portholes strengthened the main breastwork. The men worked around the clock felling trees to construct a makeshift *abatis*, or barricade, in front of both earthworks and to block the turnpike and the old wagon road to Sublett Ford. Moore then placed four companies of the Twenty-fifth Michigan inside the earthworks, leaving one company in reserve, and positioned the Eighth Michigan and Seventy-ninth New York detachments above the river bridge in the rear. By the morning of July 4, the Union defenses at the narrows of Tebbs Bend were complete.

The Confederates moved out at daybreak on what promised to be a hot, sunny day. Although his division could easily bypass the Federal enclave, Morgan felt he could not leave Moore's troops in his rear. Morgan had complete confidence that he could capture the post. "It was his practice to attack and seek to capture all, but the strongest, of the forces which opposed his advance upon his raids," Duke said. In reality, Morgan was unaware of the strength of the enemy position. Captain Franks had not studied the layout of the enemy's earthworks, nor had he been able to estimate the size of Moore's force. Nevertheless, the lack of information would not deter the general from executing his plan. Morgan sent portions of Johnson's and

Duke's brigades on a flanking maneuver to get into the rear of the Federals. These Confederate regiments forded the Green River at Lemmons Bend before settling on the north end of the Green River Bridge. Meanwhile, Morgan deployed the main column into a line of battle facing the rifle pit. Moore found himself surrounded, but this did not discourage him. He was anxious to fight.

Captain Byrne opened the battle at 6:30 a.m. with a few shells thrown from one of his Parrott guns. The cannon shots scored a direct hit on the Union forward rifle pit, wounding a few of the defenders. Morgan ceased fire and sent Lieutenant Colonel Alston forward with a flag of truce. Alston bore Colonel Moore a brief message from General Morgan. It read, "Sir, in the name of the Confederate States Government, I demand an immediate and unconditional surrender of the entire force under your command, together with the stockade. I am, Very Respectfully, Jno. H. Morgan, Comdg. Division Cav. C.S.A." Colonel Moore replied with a grin, "Present my compliments to General Morgan, and say to him that, this being the fourth day of July, I cannot entertain his proposition."

About 7:30 a.m., Morgan ordered the four guns of Byrne's Battery to let loose. The cannons roared as the shell fell heavily on the forward rifle pit, but the seventy-five men in the trench held firm. Sharpshooters in the main breastwork took aim at the Rebel artillerymen; within a short time, nearly a dozen of Byrne's men were shot down, and one of the guns was disabled. The snipers made the area around the battery too perilous for Byrne's cannoneers, forcing them to take cover. The battery went silent.

Undaunted, Morgan ordered Colonel Johnson to storm the rifle pit with Chenault's Eleventh Kentucky Cavalry and Huffman's Seventh Kentucky Cavalry. About 9:30 a.m., the regiments dismounted and formed into line. With a Rebel yell, the men rushed forward across the open field. Company A, Tenth Kentucky Cavalry, accompanied them on their right flank. They quickly overran the rifle pit and its occupants, who fell back to the safety of the primary breastwork. Morgan's assault column took shelter in the rifle pit and the thick woods on each flank.

Morgan joined Colonel Johnson in the captured Union rifle pit. After surveying the main Union fortification, Morgan ordered Johnson to assault the fort without artillery support. "I begged the general not to attempt it," Johnson bemoaned, "as I had but seven rounds of ammunition and we could easily flank the place; but he insisted and I led my men to the charge." Duke would follow up Johnson's attack with Smith's Fifth Kentucky Cavalry, who were lined up behind a stable to the rear. The charge was sounded, and

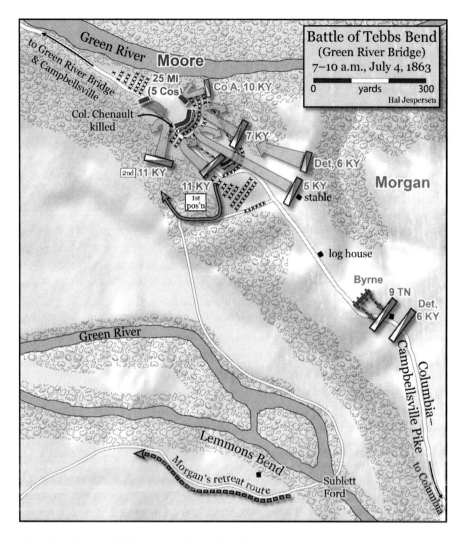

Map of the Battle of Tebbs Bend (Green River Bridge), located eight miles south of Campbellsville, Kentucky. *Author's collection.*

Johnson's and Smith's men advanced at the double-quick across a narrow field. Moore's men responded with an accurate sustained fire on the Rebel line. The raiders dropped in large numbers. As they reached the *abatis* in front of the fortification, they were exposed even more to the death borne from the Michiganders' rifles, but the raiders poured their deadly pistol and rifle fire into the stockade. "The bullets flew from all sides," wrote Private Dirk Van Raalte. "Sometimes we and the Rebs were only six or eight feet from each other." The raiders found they could not penetrate beyond the *abatis* and ditch of the fort. They withdrew to the relative safety of the woods along the bluffs, leaving a bloody trail of dead and wounded soldiers lying propped against the felled trees or sprawled in the field.

The Confederates regrouped to renew the attack while Morgan ordered Colonel David W. Chenault to make a flank attack on the Federal fortification. Chenault led the remnants of his Eleventh Kentucky down the south bluff toward the river and then climbed back up the bluff through the thick woods. When they reached the edge of the clearing in the right rear of the Union fortification, Chenault leaped forward on his horse, and his men followed him on foot up the slope. The Fifth, Sixth and Seventh Kentucky supported them with another charge across the open field. Duke watched in horror as the assaults were cut to pieces: "The first rush carried the men close to the work, but they were stopped by the fallen timber, and dropped fast under the close fire of the enemy. Colonel Chenault was killed in the midst of the abattis [*sic*]—his brains blown out as he was firing his pistol into the earthwork and calling on his men to follow...Colonel Smith led his men at a double-quick to the abattis, where they were stopped as the others had been, and suffered severely." Major Thomas Y. Brent Jr., a favorite of the Fifth Kentucky, fell dead when he ran over to help Chenault. Captain Alexander Tribble and an alarming number of junior grade officers met the same fate. Just as Chenault's men gained the turnpike, Moore's reserve company of the Twenty-fifth Michigan smashed into their flank and pushed the Confederates back down the bluff. After suffering heavy casualties, Morgan's attack stalled. The beaten raiders withdrew to the cover of the woods.

As the fighting at the earthworks wound down about 10:00 a.m., the Eighth and Tenth Kentucky charged Moore's soldiers at the bridge. Moore's Michigan and New York infantrymen released a volley that unhorsed some of the riders. The Confederates fell back. The Kentuckians resolved they could not capture the bridge and returned to the main column to report the situation to General Morgan.

At 10:30 a.m., Morgan sent in a flag of truce to attend to the dead and wounded. Moore counted six killed and twenty-four wounded. Morgan's casualties were much heavier. He suffered thirty-six killed, forty-five wounded and thirty-two captured in less than thirty minutes of total combat. Duke appreciated his foe's compassion for the fallen raiders: "Our wounded and dead were left under the charge of Surgeons and Chaplains, who received every assistance, that he could furnish, from Colonel Moore, who proved himself as humane as he was skillful and gallant." The Kentucky legislature

Confederate major James B. McCreary took temporary command of the Eleventh Kentucky Cavalry when his superior, Lieutenant Colonel Tucker, fell ill on the Great Raid. After the war, McCreary was elected twice as governor of Kentucky and six times to the U.S. Congress. *Courtesy of Cowan's Auctions Inc., Cincinnati, Ohio.*

later wrote two resolutions congratulating Moore on his victory at Tebbs Bend. General Burnside also thanked Moore, but General Boyle never said a word.

The raiders considered the Battle of Tebbs Bend the worst fight they had experienced in the war up to that time. Nearly all agreed the battle had been a useless effusion of blood. John Weatherred of the Ninth Tennessee Cavalry wrote in his diary, "It was foolish to attack, most of us thought." Morgan's overconfidence had bested him again. Looking back at the disaster at Tebbs Bend, Johnson said, "Had the enemy's force in our rear used ordinary diligence, they could have given us trouble at this place."

Morgan turned his column toward the rear and crossed the Green River at Sublett Ford and the other fords of Lemmons Bend used earlier in the day. After gaining the north side of the river, they picked up the Columbia–Campbellsville Pike and followed it through Campbellsville, interrupting the town's Independence Day celebrations. The raiders continued northward, drove off the enemy's pickets and camped for the night around the village of New Market, four miles south of Lebanon. Leeland Hathaway remarked that "General Morgan looked haggard and weary, but he never despaired." July 4, 1863—the day Pemberton surrendered Vicksburg to Grant and the day Lee began his retreat south from the bloody battlefield at Gettysburg—had proven to be a terrible day for Morgan's men, too. Major James B. McCreary of the Eleventh Kentucky scribbled his thoughts in his journal that night: "It was a sad, sorrowful day, and more tears of grief rolled over my weather beaten cheeks on this mournful occasion than have before for years. The commencement of this raid is ominous."

The downtrodden soldiers lying about their campfires requested for nineteen-year-old Lieutenant Tom Morgan, the general's youngest brother, to serenade them. While Tom soulfully sang "We Sat by the River, You and I," his beautiful tenor voice brought tears to the eyes of many of his battle-hardened comrades. Leeland Hathaway somberly noted, "So plaintive and sweet were the notes that it would have been a fitting requiem for the dead."

On the foggy morning of July 5, Morgan's raiders broke camp and headed toward Lebanon, a Union supply depot defended by a garrison of 380 men under Lieutenant Colonel Charles S. Hanson. Morgan not only wanted to suppress this enemy position, but also his men needed the supplies for the journey ahead. Morgan marched his division over three roads that converged on Lebanon from the west and south. The advance troopers engaged the Union pickets on all three roads. After some sharp skirmishing, the Confederates slowly pushed the enemy toward Lebanon.

Charles Hanson was the brother of Confederate brigadier general Roger W. Hanson, who had been killed at the Battle of Stones River. Charley claimed many friends and relatives who were now members of Morgan's command. At 6:00 p.m. on Independence Day, Burnside had telegraphed Hanson with the order to "select some defensible position and hold out if attacked until re-enforcements came, and not to let the enemy take you." Since then, Hanson had received dispatches from his scouts that confirmed the enemy greatly outnumbered his garrison, but he was determined to hold the town until reinforcements arrived from Danville.

Hanson's force consisted of his own Twentieth Kentucky (U.S.) Infantry regiment and small detachments from three other regiments, including an undersized company from the Ninth Kentucky (U.S.) Cavalry. The Twentieth Kentucky had fought at Shiloh and Perryville, and its men were itching for some action. Like their leader, many of the men had family or friends in Morgan's command. The colonel readied his soldiers for the fight sure to come in the morning. They built a barricade of wagons across the Campbellsville Pike on the outskirts of town and placed a twenty-four-pounder cannon in the road. Hanson selected various public buildings and houses in town to be used as fortresses when his troops were driven in. If those buildings were to fall, he instructed his officers to converge on the brick Louisville & Nashville Railroad depot located on Depot Street. After all orders had been issued, he stretched his Twentieth Kentucky into a skirmish line from the St. Mary's Pike over to the Bradfordsville Pike, where the small detachment from the Ninth Kentucky anchored the left flank.

When the Confederate advance on the Campbellsville Pike reached a point about one and a half miles from town, Morgan deployed his brigades as skirmishers across an impressive-looking two-mile front stretching from the St. Mary's Pike to the Bradfordsville Pike. Captain Byrne placed his artillery on Bricken's Hill near the center of the line at the Campbellsville Pike. About 7:00 a.m., Morgan ordered three guns of Byrne's Battery to open fire on the Union line. Repeating the pattern he had followed at Tebbs Bend and at many previous battlefields, Morgan sent Lieutenant Colonel Alston with a flag of truce toward the town. Morgan hoped to avoid bloodshed, especially when their Kentucky brothers' lives were at stake. After nearly getting shot accidently, Alston delivered to Hanson a demand to surrender unconditionally. The Union commander politely refused. As Alston was leaving, he warned Hanson to evacuate the women and children of the town before the bombardment resumed.

Before Hanson could move the civilians out of harm's way, Byrne's four guns lobbed shells toward the Union line. Two of the guns took aim at the depot, while the other two fired into the streets. Some shells hit the roof of the depot; others struck the Presbyterian Church steeple, while others landed on the lawn of Spaulding's plantation home. Morgan gave the command to attack, and the long line of Confederate skirmishers steadily tramped forward over the intervening fields. The gray wave appeared to grow larger the nearer it came to town, as if it were about to gobble up the defenders. When the enemy came within range, Hanson's Kentuckians let loose a volley that staggered the Confederates momentarily. On they came, but Hanson's veterans put up a good fight. "My skirmishers fought desperately for two hours in the open field, protected by fences and wagons and other temporary obstructions," wrote Hanson. "Being overpowered, they fell back." Captain Frank E. Wolcott, who led the detachments of the Twentieth Kentucky and Ninth Kentucky in the Bradfordsville Pike sector, conducted a gallant street fight against the Ninth Tennessee and Sixth Kentucky. Wolcott's bluecoats slowly gave ground until they barricaded themselves in the Harris House and livery and in some adjacent buildings near Main and Market Streets. From there, they held off their rival Kentuckians and Tennesseans for nearly four hours until they were forced to fall back toward the houses near the depot.

Meanwhile, the Fourteenth Kentucky Cavalry charged down the Campbellsville Pike. The Eighth Kentucky joined them on their left. They broke through the barricade, dispersed its Union defenders and captured the Union cannon before it could fire a shot. On the left, Johnson's brigade easily outflanked its opponents on the St. Mary's Pike. The Yankees retreated from

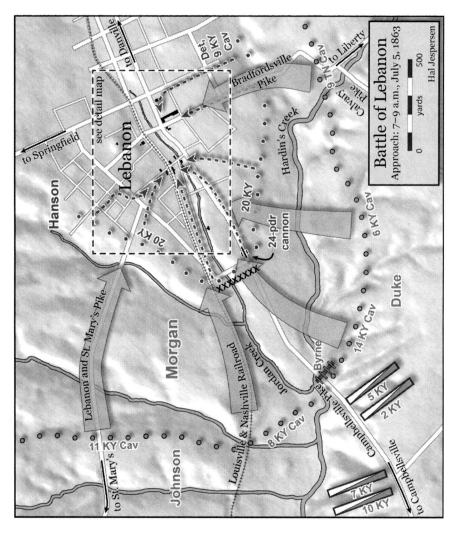

Map of the Battle of Lebanon, Kentucky, showing Morgan's advance on the town. *Author's collection.*

this position to the safety of the fortified buildings north of the depot, while the Union soldiers withdrew from the Campbellsville Pike sector into the depot, commissary building and private dwellings south of the depot.

The depot, Hanson's primary stronghold, quickly became the center of attention. Morgan ordered the Eighth Kentucky and Fourteenth Kentucky to make an assault on the depot. The mounted soldiers galloped across the open ground on the south and west sides of the building, but Hanson's defenders, poking their guns out of the depot's windows and doors, riddled the Confederates with bullets. Captain Tom Franks, the recently appointed leader of Morgan's scouts, cried, "I am killed!" and fell severely wounded. Leeland Hathaway counted seven bullet holes in his clothes, but miraculously each missile had missed his body. The attack was stopped cold, and the men dropped to the ground to take cover.

The exchange of gunfire became rapid and incessant. Hanson's men played havoc on the Confederates who lay prone in the fields around the railroad yard. "The calmness and business-like composure of my men, added to their superior skill in the use of the Enfield and Springfield rifles at long range, saved the building in which we had taken refuge, by keeping the enemy's artillery at least 1,000 yards off," remembered Hanson. "Many of the enemy were killed at a distance of 400 and a few as far as 900 yards." Despite a hail of Union lead, Private Walter Ferguson of the Fourteenth Kentucky sprinted across the field to carry off his messmate, Private Tom Logwood, who was badly wounded. After a couple hours of close-quarters fighting in over ninety-degree heat, the Eleventh Kentucky, Seventh Kentucky and Tenth Kentucky neutralized the buildings and houses north of the depot, but they remained pinned down outside the north and east walls of the depot and commissary.

At noon, Morgan called a cease-fire to send in another flag of truce; this time, it was brought in by citizens of the town. Morgan's message stated that if Hanson did not surrender, the town would be burned and no quarter would be shown to the Federals. However, the message never reached Hanson at the depot. When he spotted Lieutenant Elias D. Lawrence wheeling one of his Parrotts onto Sunnyside Hill, within three hundred yards of the depot, Hanson ordered his men to resume firing. Lawrence opened up on the depot. Before the day's end, twenty-six solid shot and shell would penetrate the depot's roof and set it on fire. The depot's second floor was essentially reduced to rubble, but because Hanson's troops occupied the first floor, they remained unharmed. The fighting raged with ferocity. An hour later, the Sixth Kentucky and Ninth Tennessee dislodged Wolcott's men, who retreated through the streets into the houses near the depot. This allowed the Sixth Kentucky and Ninth Tennessee to concentrate their fire on the south side of the depot.

Morgan was running out of time. He had a tough decision to make. He had learned from the Tenth Kentucky pickets that a large Union force was only three miles away on the Danville road. He could either disengage from the battle or he could charge the depot again. He chose the latter. Morgan called on the best street-fighting unit in the division, Major Thomas

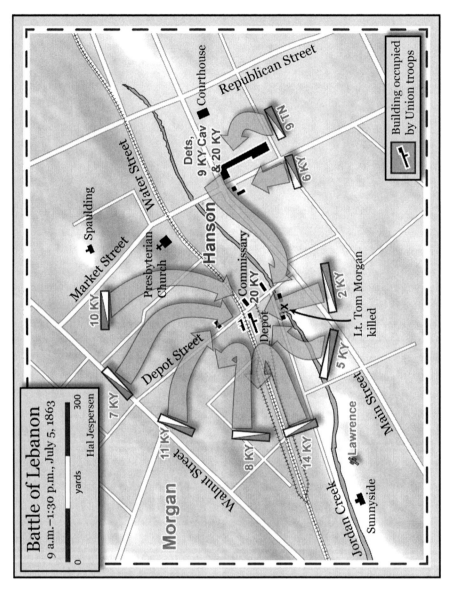

Map of the Battle of Lebanon, Kentucky, showing the desperate street fighting in town. *Author's collection.*

Webber's Second Kentucky Cavalry, to storm the south side of the depot. Joining Webber's regiment on the west side would be Smith's Fifth Kentucky Cavalry. Webber's men were fresh, having waited in reserve up to this time. The men dismounted for the assault. When the charge was sounded just after 1:00 p.m., the cavalrymen rushed forward with a Rebel yell. Colonel D. Howard Smith, on horseback and waving his hat, urged his soldiers forward across the rail yard. Webber's men surged around the fortified houses on Main Street and struck the south side of the depot. Private Bennett H. Young of the Eighth Kentucky, who had been pinned down near the depot for hours, said the charge of the Second Kentucky was one of the bravest things he had witnessed during the war. "It required almost superhuman courage to undertake this act, yet it was done with a calmness that would thrill every observer," he remembered. Running ahead of his comrades, with a pistol blazing in his hand, the recklessly brave Lieutenant Tom Morgan cheered the men forward. Just then, rifles flashed from within the depot, and a bullet plowed into Tom's chest. Young Tom fell into his older brother Calvin's arms. "Brother Cally, they have killed me." With those words, Tom died.

Upon hearing of Tom's death, General Morgan became enraged. He ordered the buildings surrounding the depot to be burned. Fires broke out while the Second and Fifth Kentucky shot directly into the windows of the depot, pushing the defenders back into the interior. At 1:20 p.m., Hanson raised the white flag after he spotted flames and heard the Rebels' threats to burn the whole town.

By now, word had spread about Tom Morgan's death. The loss of one of their most beloved comrades sent a shock wave through the division. The men's distress came to a head during the surrender proceedings. As the prisoners were being led out of the depot, Captain Charlton Morgan, another of the general's brothers, grabbed Hanson's beard and yelled in his face, "I'll blow your brains out, you damned rascal!" Colonel D. Howard Smith, an old childhood friend of Hanson's, helped calm Charlton down. Some of the raiders threatened to kill their captives, but General Morgan, with tears welling up in his eyes, pulled his pistol with the promise to shoot the first man who harmed a prisoner. Then, turning to Hanson, the general said, "Charles, when you go home, if it is any source of gratification to you, tell Mother you killed brother Tom." With this, the death threats subsided.

The Confederate rank and file took out their frustrations on the citizens. Twenty of Lebanon's buildings and houses, many owned by Union sympathizers, were destroyed during and after the battle. The county clerk's office and the depot were among those that went up in flames. Meanwhile, the raiders pilfered many of the town's businesses. Morgan's Division was able to resupply itself with horses, guns, ammunition, clothes, accoutrements and wagons from the captured military stores at Lebanon. Captain Sidney P. Cunningham, Morgan's assistant adjutant general, reported that they destroyed the captured twenty-four-pounder cannon.

Hanson lost 3 killed, 16 wounded (1 mortally) and 360 captured in the Battle of Lebanon. The men of the Twentieth Kentucky later claimed it was their toughest fight of the war. Morgan's Division recorded 13 killed, 26 wounded (2 mortally) and 17 captured. The fratricidal battle—Kentuckian against Kentuckian, brother against brother—had cost both sides dearly, but none more than General Morgan. That night, his brother Tom's body was laid out at Sunnyside, and soldiers from both sides came to pay their respects. They buried Tom in the rose garden at Sunnyside. Alston summed up the day in his diary: "July 5—Another day of gloom, fatigue, and death."

With the appearance of Colonel James I. David's force of Michigan cavalry and artillery just outside Lebanon, Morgan had no time to parole the prisoners. He had already been delayed seven hours by Hanson's stubborn defense. The raiders rode out of town on the Springfield Pike about 3:30 p.m., herding the Federal soldiers with them. Despite the sweltering heat, the prisoners were force-marched at the double-quick the eight miles to Springfield. The raiders, still smarting from the loss of their comrades at Tebbs Bend and Lebanon, treated their captives badly. Many stole personal items and clothes from the prisoners, including shoes and hats. Several of the Union soldiers died from heat exhaustion or from being trampled over by the artillery. One Confederate brained a prisoner with the butt of his gun and killed him. A sudden severe thunderstorm cooled the air and doused the men's anger, saving many prisoners' lives. After reaching the relative safety of Springfield at nightfall, Morgan had the prisoners paroled and released while the Confederate column pushed on through the dark toward Bardstown.

Lieutenant Colonel Hanson blamed the loss at Lebanon on Colonel David for failing to come to his rescue. Neither Hanson nor some of David's own subordinates could understand why it had taken David over four hours to cover the last three miles to Lebanon and why he had failed to attack Morgan's rear guard when the opportunity presented itself. However, General Burnside saw things differently. With his own frustration building over the poor performance of Judah, and not yet knowing all the facts, Burnside condemned Hanson for surrendering Lebanon. Burnside relieved the lieutenant colonel of his command and ordered his arrest for dereliction of duty. A week later, Burnside admitted his mistake and rescinded the order.

Confederate captain Ralph Sheldon, one of the original members of the Old Squadron, led Company C of the Second Kentucky Cavalry in the last charge of the Great Raid. He was captured with Morgan at West Point, Ohio. *Courtesy of Cowan's Auctions Inc., Cincinnati, Ohio.*

After paroling the prisoners, Lieutenant Colonel Robert Alston sent Captain William J. Davis ahead to find his command while he took a brief rest at the Cunningham house in Springfield. Cold, hungry and exhausted, Alston fell asleep. The next morning, his orderly awakened him, and they raced off in the direction of Bardstown to catch up with the column. Several miles down the road, they unexpectedly ran into a Union patrol and were captured. "My God! How I hated it, no one can understand," Alston lamented. "My first thought, after my wife and children, was my fine mare, Fannie Johnson, named after a pretty little cousin, of Richmond, Va...I turned her over to the [enemy] captain and begged him to take good care of her, which he promised to do." Alston's raid was over, and now Morgan was without his dependable chief of staff.

Before arriving at Lebanon, Morgan had sent Captain Ralph Sheldon with his Company C, Second Kentucky Cavalry, on a special mission. Sheldon was to scout in the direction of Louisville to gain necessary intelligence about enemy troop movements. When finished, Sheldon would rendezvous with the main column at Bardstown. However, he ran into an unexpected snag that cost him a whole day.

That snag came in the form of Lieutenant Thomas W. Sullivan and twenty-five men of the Fourth U.S. Cavalry. On the morning of July 5, Sullivan's detachment collided with some scouts from Sheldon's company on the Louisville Road about six miles north of Bardstown. Sullivan charged them at a gallop and drove them beyond the town. By this time, his horses were tired, and he fell back to Bardstown to rest them. When he reached town, he learned Sheldon's men were approaching in force. Sullivan immediately barricaded his men inside Humphreys's livery stable, in which they piled boards and manure into a mound to cover the gate.

About 11:30 a.m., Sheldon mounted a charge on three sides of the livery. Lieutenant Sullivan's troopers inside the building killed two of the raiders before Sheldon withdrew his men to a safe distance. Private Bartholomew Burke, Company H, Fourth U.S. Cavalry, was hit during the exchange. As Burke collapsed to the ground, he called out to his commander, "Lieutenant, did I fall like a soldier?" Those were his last words. Sheldon sent in a flag of truce demanding the Federals' surrender. Sullivan refused, saying, "I hope to gain the esteem of General Morgan by a gallant defense."

The firing quickly resumed, and a siege ensued. The Confederates surrounded the entire city block in which the livery was located. At one point, Sheldon ordered a team to set the stable on fire, but Sullivan's troopers killed two of the Confederates who made the failed attempt. The raiders roped off all the streets and alleys to prevent Sullivan's men from sneaking out under cover of darkness. Colonel Richard Morgan arrived later that night with his Fourteenth Kentucky Cavalry, bolstering Sheldon's positions around the block. With the Rebels perched behind fence corners, houses, buildings and the adjoining Salem Baptist Church, the area around the stable became a no-man's land as sniping between the opposing forces continued throughout the night.

At 4:00 a.m. on July 6, the head of General Morgan's main column trudged into Bardstown. Soon, Colonel Richard C. Morgan instructed Captain Sheldon to escort another flag of truce to the besieged Federals. He demanded an immediate and unconditional surrender of the garrison or else he would "blow them to hell with his artillery." Again, Sullivan declined, saying, "I am obliged to the general for his kind intentions, and feel sorry that it becomes my duty to trouble him a little longer." Frustrated, Colonel Morgan ordered his men to open a brisk fire on the stable while he brought up Captain Byrne's artillery. As the four guns were rolled into place at point-

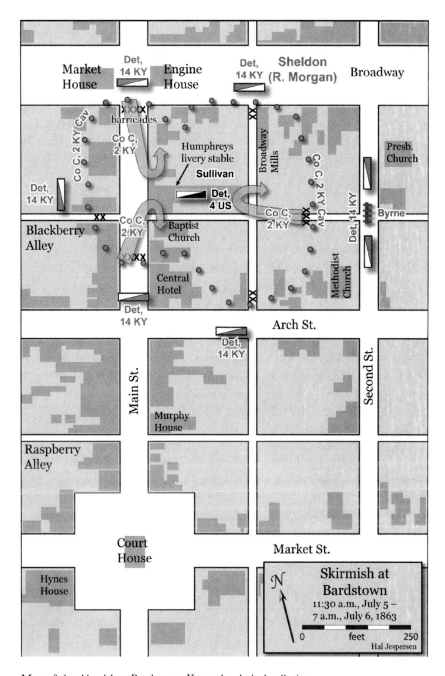

Map of the skirmish at Bardstown, Kentucky. *Author's collection.*

blank range from the stable, a Union sentry on the roof reported the bad news to the lieutenant.

Knowing the game was up, Sullivan walked out of the stable door about 7:00 a.m. with a white flag in his hand. The Rebels shot at him, much to the disgust of the residents watching the scene unfold. Colonel Morgan did not accept the lieutenant's surrender at first: "Go back; you have refused these terms twice; you have no right to demand them now." Just as the Confederate guards manhandled Sullivan back through the stable door, Colonel Morgan, realizing every hour was precious, recanted his decision. This time he took Sullivan's gallant detachment prisoners, "although [Sullivan] did not deserve it on account of [his] foolish and stubborn resistance." Later, after being briefed about the fight, General Morgan "could not help complimenting the 25 'damned Yankees' who detained him twenty-four hours."

With Bardstown being less than forty miles from the Federal stronghold at Louisville, Boyle and Burnside assumed Morgan would target the city and its rich supply of war materiel. Such a plan had been discussed among Confederate military gurus for quite some time, and Union authorities were well aware of it. Burnside was quite upset by the poor performance of his field commanders over the previous three days. Because Judah had reacted ineptly, the raiders were now within a day's ride of one of the Union army's most valuable supply depots. If Morgan broke through Louisville's defenses and destroyed its military warehouses, Burnside's career would be jeopardized.

Morgan had no intention of attacking Louisville, but he would use the fear within the Union high command as a tool to hide his real destination. Morgan sent multiple detachments, including two companies under Captain William Davis, toward Harrodsburg and Louisville to deceive Union authorities into thinking he was planning to strike those places. Leaving Bardstown on July 6, Davis and his detachment successfully skirted Louisville, forced a crossing of the Ohio River at Twelve Mile Island and terrorized southern Indiana before they were captured near Pekin on July 11.

Morgan called on his master telegrapher, George A. "Lightning" Ellsworth, to determine the enemy's response to these diversions. Canadian-born "Lightning" Ellsworth could intercept enemy telegrams with ease. Although he did not make a good soldier, he made up for it with his exceptional skills employing the telegraph. He also harbored a talent for memorizing the tapping rhythm, or "fist," of a telegraph operator by simply listening to the operator's style for a short time. Telegraph station attendants recognized one another's tapping rhythms and, therefore, could identify an imposter on the wire fairly

George A. "Lightning" Ellsworth, Morgan's master telegrapher and early pioneer of electronic counterintelligence. Ellsworth escaped from Ohio and survived the war. He worked with inventor Thomas Edison in Cincinnati but was killed in a gunfight in Texas. *Photo from* Confederate Veteran Magazine *(November 5, 1897).*

easily. Ellsworth's talent allowed him to pose as a Union telegraph operator. In this role, he would send deceptive messages to Union headquarters. In the messages, he would say Morgan was somewhere that he was not or that he was going somewhere that he would not. Ellsworth would often falsify the actual strength of Morgan's force to a number many times larger, which would convince Union authorities to keep their troops stationary for defense. Ellsworth's messages created confusion and indecision at Union headquarters. His activities constituted one of the earliest forms of electronic warfare.

On the night of July 6, Morgan instructed Ellsworth to work his magic at Bardstown Junction. George tapped into the wires and listened intently to telegraph exchanges between Union operators. The telegrams surmised that Morgan's intended direction was north—to Louisville. Of course, they were wrong. Morgan headed west. Before leaving Bardstown Junction, Morgan's advance guard drove a portion of Captain Daniel Morris's Company C, Sixty-third Indiana Infantry, toward Shepherdsville in a running skirmish that resulted in one Union soldier killed and two captured. Two raiders were killed. Afterward, Morgan's troopers destroyed Bardstown Junction's stockade, burned a trestle and a water tank house of the Louisville & Nashville Railroad and captured a train containing Lieutenant William F. Henderson and thirty men from the Sixty-third Indiana Infantry.

Meanwhile, Hobson started in pursuit of Morgan with all the nearest mobile units he could find. He was thoroughly frustrated by Judah's poor decisions during the critical hours following the Cumberland River crossings. In the early morning of July 6, Hobson led his mounted regiments from their camp at Greensburg, Kentucky, and galloped into Campbellsville by daybreak. General Shackelford awaited him there with his own brigade of cavalry. They combined their forces and rode off toward Lebanon. When they arrived in town, they found Colonel Wolford and his troopers measuring up the mess that had been made by Morgan's Division the day before. Wolford's regiments joined with Hobson's and Shackelford's brigades. Soon thereafter, Judah issued another ridiculous order to send the infantry and the Twenty-second Indiana Battery to him; Hobson reluctantly obeyed.

After hearing of Hobson's actions, Burnside sent an order to Hobson at 4:30 p.m. on July 6 to take command of all mounted troops in the region and chase after Morgan. Burnside's directive essentially gave Hobson leadership over Judah's troops, even though Judah was his superior. When Colonel August Kautz's brigade arrived later that day, Hobson merged it with the other brigades to form the Provisional Division, totaling about 2,500 cavalry and mounted infantry with six pieces of artillery. From this point onward, the Provisional Division would be the enemy force most feared by Morgan and his troopers.

PROVISIONAL CAVALRY DIVISION (July 6–21, 1863)* Brig. Gen. Edward H. Hobson		
Kautz's Brigade Col. August V. Kautz	Wolford's Brigade Col. Frank L. Wolford	Shackelford's Brigade Brig. Gen. James M. Shackelford
2nd Ohio Cavalry, Lt. Col. George A. Purington	1st Kentucky (U.S.) Cavalry, Lt. Col. Silas Adams	3rd Kentucky (U.S.) Cavalry (1 bttn.), Maj. Lewis W. Wolfley
7th Ohio Cavalry, Col. Israel Garrard	2nd East Tennessee (Mounted) Infantry, Lt. Col. James M. Melton	8th Kentucky (U.S.) Cavalry, Col. Benjamin H. Bristow (Lt. Col. James H. Holloway, beginning July 15, 1863)
	45th Ohio (Mounted) Infantry, Lt. Col. George E. Ross	9th Kentucky (U.S.) Cavalry, Col. Richard T. Jacob

		12th Kentucky (U.S.) Cavalry, Col. Eugene W. Crittenden
Hammond's Battery [attached to 65th Indiana (Mounted) Infantry (Co. K)] (two guns) Capt. John W. Hammond		
Law's Kentucky (U.S.) Mountain Howitzer Battery (four 12-pounder mountain howitzers) Lt. Jesse S. Law		

*Col. William P. Sanders's brigade would join Hobson's division on July 15, 1863. Sanders's brigade consisted of the 8th Michigan Cavalry (10 cos.), Lt. Col. Grover S. Wormer; 9th Michigan Cavalry (Cos. A, B, F and L), Lt. Col. George S. Acker; and two rifled guns of Battery L, 1st Michigan Light Artillery [11th Michigan Battery], Lt. Cyrus D. Roys.

Morgan's Division rode through the night and reached Garnettsville, Kentucky, on the afternoon of July 7. While the men rested, a small contingent of scouts under Captain Sam Taylor and Captain Clay Meriwether casually rode into the peaceful river town of Brandenburg. There they met Captain Thomas Hines and a dozen of his men from the Ninth Kentucky Cavalry. They were all that remained of an eighty-man detachment that Hines had led on a clandestine raid into Indiana over the previous three weeks. Although his losses had been frightful, the value of the information Hines had gathered would be immeasurable for Morgan's Division.

In the late afternoon of the same day, Hobson sent an urgent telegram from Bardstown Junction. "I communicated with Brigadier General Boyle, commanding District of Kentucky," reported Hobson, "advising him of the move of Morgan toward Brandenburg, and requested that a gunboat be sent to that place to prevent him crossing the river into Indiana." Boyle never acted on this message. When Confederate scouts arrived in Brandenburg, the U.S. Navy was nowhere to be found. Morgan's feints had been successful. No Union troops or U.S. Navy gunboats blocked Morgan's passage to the Hoosier state. Private steamboats plowed the waters of the Ohio River like on any normal day. None of their captains realized Morgan's men were so close.

Confederate captain Thomas Hines of the Ninth Kentucky Cavalry served as one of Morgan's best spies. Hines gathered intelligence in Indiana prior to the Great Raid. Escaping prison, he led several more covert operations. He became a chief justice of the Kentucky Court of Appeals. *From* History of Kentucky *by Connelley and Coulter (1922).*

Meriwether and Taylor's scouting party went promptly to work. They asked a Confederate sympathizer to hail the Louisville packet *John T. McCombs* toward the Brandenburg wharf. After it landed, the scouts boarded the steamboat at gunpoint like the pirates of the high seas. After releasing the passengers, they forced the pilot to anchor the steamboat in the middle of the Ohio River. When another steamboat, the *Alice Dean*, approached Brandenburg, the scouts hoisted a distress signal from the *John T. McCombs*. Responding to the packet's apparent plea for help, the *Alice Dean* moved up alongside it. The raiders jumped aboard and lashed the two steamboats together. Soldiers waving their pistols in the air were enough to convince Captain James Pepper to surrender his boat.

The capture of the *John T. McCombs* and the *Alice Dean* was a stroke of good fortune for Morgan. Now he could transport his men, horses, artillery and wagons across the river quickly and safely. With Hobson only a day's ride behind him, Morgan needed to cross the Ohio River as fast as possible or else he might find himself trapped in Brandenburg with the river at his back.

On the evening of the seventh, some Unionist citizens hurried two miles downriver to Mauckport, Indiana, to report Morgan's presence to Lieutenant Colonel William J. Irvin, commander of a local detachment of the Indiana Legion militia. Irvin immediately sent a courier to Colonel Lewis Jordon, stationed at Corydon, Indiana, to alert him of the situation. Meanwhile, Irvin commandeered the steamboat *Lady Pike* to transport 30 men of

Colonel Woodbury's Leavenworth Home Guard detachment and Captain George W. Lyon's six-pounder three-inch rifled cannon. They arrived at Mauckport about midnight, from which place they marched overland to Morvin's Landing, a defunct steamboat landing located directly opposite Brandenburg. Colonel John Timberlake and three companies of the Sixth Indiana Legion joined them. The 130 militiamen and single cannon were in line along the north bank of the Ohio River by 7:00 a.m. on July 8.

Morgan's main column broke camp about midnight and marched into Brandenburg about 9:00 a.m. on July 8. Up to this point, they had put 175 miles behind them, but they looked forward to traveling many more in the land north of the Ohio River. "As we looked on the river, rolling before us, we felt that it divided us from a momentous future, and we were eager to learn our fate," wrote Duke. General Morgan gave Captain Hines the ravaged position of head of scouts, which, over the course of six days, had been occupied by three previous officers who were now casualties.

Irvin had ordered Lyon to direct his cannon fire at the boilers and machinery of the two captured steamboats, but Timberlake countermanded the order. Instead, he instructed Lyon to aim at the Rebels along the Brandenburg wharf. With a dense fog shrouding his location, Lyon opened fire on the unsuspecting troopers lined up along the landing. The first shot passed through the upper rigging of the *John T. McCombs*. Three members of the Fourteenth Kentucky were killed and several wounded before the rest ran for cover in a ravine behind the town. During a lull, Colonel Timberlake yelled from across the water, "I demand you to surrender and bring those boats over here in the name of the United States and the State of Indiana!" One of the Rebels on the wharf answered, "Oh hell, old man, come over and take a drink." Lyon resumed his work. As the enemy shells rained down on the Brandenburg riverfront, Private Curtis R. Burke remembered a frightened woman crying out, "Oh, is this war! Are you going to have a battle?"

Timberlake's infantrymen raised their rifles and unleashed a volley on the boats, but the enemy's position was too far away to do any damage. Captain Byrne quickly responded to the threat by deploying four guns on the low hill on which sat the courthouse. When the fog lifted, Byrne's more accurate guns released their shells on the militiamen with singular effect. The third shell struck an abandoned cabin adjacent to the Union cannon, rattling the nerves of the militiamen who were under fire for the first time. They broke for Home Guard Canyon, a wooded swale bisecting the cleared bottomland about halfway between the landing and the bluffs. They tried to bring the six-pounder with them, but Byrne's fire scattered the frightened men, who

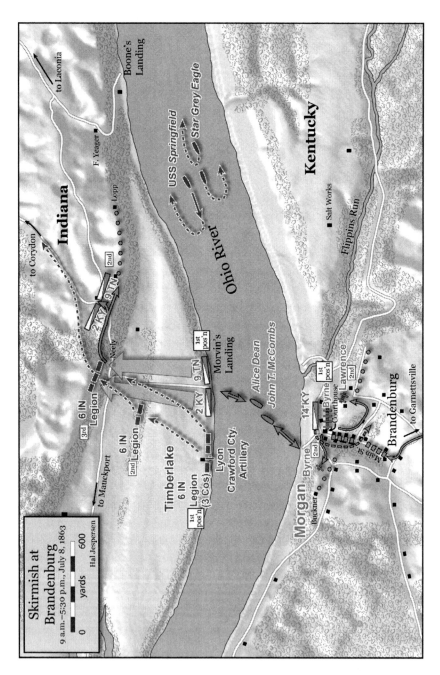

Map of the skirmish at Brandenburg, Kentucky. *Author's collection.*

had to move the cannon by hand. The piece for some time stood alone at the bank until some courageous militiamen came back to man the gun, but soon after, it was abandoned.

Meanwhile, the Ninth Tennessee Cavalry and Second Kentucky Cavalry boarded the *John T. McCombs* and the *Alice Dean*, which ferried them across the Ohio River to Morvin's Landing. The men could not bring their horses for lack of room on the steamboats; their steeds would cross on another trip. As the boats steamed toward the north bank, the militiamen fired on them, and the Rebels on board fired back. "They fired at us with a cannon, made it hail against the boat [*John T. McCombs*]," remembered Private Weatherred of the Ninth Tennessee. "As this boat landed we jumped ashore and forward in line in about 5 minutes and charged them, they ran into the bushes back from the river and got away." Timberlake's men unleashed a volley at the dismounted cavalrymen on the bank, but the shots missed their marks. Lieutenant Lawrence then sighted his Parrotts in the direction of Home Guard Canyon. His plunging shells burst among the militiamen, killing and wounding some and forcing the rest to withdraw to a safer position on top of the high wooded river bluff. Morgan's veterans advanced steadily in line across the open bottomland, through Home Guard Canyon and up the steep wooded ridge. Before the Confederates reached the top of the bluff, Timberlake's demoralized militia retreated toward Corydon. They lost two killed and four wounded in the fight for Morvin's Landing and Home Guard Canyon, whereas the Confederates captured the ridge unscathed.

Earlier that morning, word of the Confederate presence on the Ohio River had reached Acting Ensign Joseph Watson at Portland, Kentucky. He immediately sailed off for Brandenburg in his tin-clad USS *Springfield*, armed with six twenty-four-pounder Dahlgren boat howitzers.

While the Second Kentucky and Ninth Tennessee advanced across the fields beyond Morvin's Landing, Morgan's men spotted the "curious looking craft" rounding a bend in the river toward the east. After dispersing the Union militia, the cavalrymen on the Indiana side of the river quickly formed into line along the bluff. As the *Springfield* passed below Boone's Landing, the Confederates fired into the vessel, but the gunboat was too far away for the bullets to do any harm. Ensign Watson ignored them and steamed forward. The *Springfield* let loose its guns upon Brandenburg and the cavalrymen stranded on the Indiana shore. Shot and shell crashed into buildings on Main Street but somehow missed the soldiers and civilians.

Just as the gunboat reached within a mile of Brandenburg, the Confederate artillery opened up on the *Springfield*. To get a commanding view of the river,

Byrne moved one howitzer to the bluff below town and sent Lieutenant Lawrence with his two Parrott rifles to the tall bluff above town. Lawrence's artillerymen performed good work that day, their solid shot consistently skipping over the water around the gunboat. The Parrott rifles boasted a projectile range over four times greater than that of Watson's Dahlgrens. Private Thomas Berry, watching the scene from the bluff above town, saw one of Lawrence's shells hit the pilot cabin. Being too close for comfort, Watson pulled his craft back to within the maximum range of his own artillery. Naturally, most of his shots fell short of their targets.

Colonel Duke recalled that "the duel was watched with the most breathless interest by the whole division; the men crowded in intense excitement upon the bluffs, near the town, to witness it, and General Morgan exhibited an emotion he rarely permitted to be seen." Duke was startled to see Morgan looking particularly nervous. As he surveyed the scene through his spyglass from his headquarters at the Buckner mansion, the general knew that Hobson's division was less than a day's ride behind him. Any delay of the crossing brought Hobson ever nearer. Furthermore, with two of his best regiments marooned on the Indiana shore, they could easily be attacked by overwhelming numbers of Indiana troops. Simply put, if the gunboat did not leave, the crossing would end in disaster. After exchanging fire with Lawrence's battery for nearly an hour and a half, Watson withdrew the USS *Springfield* up the river a short distance. Morgan breathed a temporary sigh of relief.

As soon as the *Springfield* disappeared around the bend, the *John T. McCombs* and the *Alice Dean* went quickly to work ferrying the horses and men across to the Indiana shore. The dismounted cavalrymen on the north bank showed "exquisite gratification" when they finally received their horses.

About 5:00 p.m., with the ferrying activity in full swing, Acting Ensign Watson and the USS *Springfield* reappeared on the scene. This time, two transport steamboats, including the *Star Grey Eagle*, accompanied the gunboat. On board the transports were five hundred Union infantrymen who had been shipped from Louisville to engage Morgan's troopers. When the Confederate artillery engaged the trio of steamboats, the transports lagged behind to avoid the deadly accurate Parrott shells. Showing confidence in the abilities of Lawrence's Parrotts, Morgan's steamboats continued shuttling troops while the duel played out. The USS *Springfield* was left by itself to suppress the enemy shore batteries, and like before, the fire from its howitzers proved ineffective. When the captains of the transports sent word that they could not find a safe place to land their troops on the Indiana shore, Watson turned the *Springfield* around, and all steamed up the river for Louisville. Lieutenant Commander Le Roy Fitch agreed with Watson's decision to retreat. "Although the *Springfield* received no injury, her commanding officer did not deem it prudent to run the batteries alone for the purpose of trying to recapture the two [captured] steamers, as, by thus doing, he ran, himself, great risks of being disabled," Fitch concluded.

It was nearly dark before the whole First Brigade stood on Hoosier soil. The Second Brigade and artillery would not be finished crossing until after midnight. The thirty-foot flames from nearby natural gas wells lit the river like giant candelabras. The artillery remained in place until the last moment when only the Eleventh Kentucky Cavalry, serving as the rear guard, was left to board. After the rear guard stepped on the enemy's shore, General Morgan looked back over the river and smiled. He had just eliminated another major barrier to his plan. He ordered the two steamboats to be burned to keep them from falling into his pursuer's hands, and then he rode away for the front of the column. The *Alice Dean* went up in flames, but Colonel Duke countermanded the order for the *John T. McCombs* because its captain was an old acquaintance. The *John T. McCombs* steamed upriver out of sight.

After the crossing had been completed, Colonel Johnson conferred with General Morgan. Before the raid had begun, Morgan had agreed that Johnson would take the Tenth Kentucky Cavalry, two artillery pieces and whatever boats they captured and operate downriver toward Evansville, while Morgan led the rest of the division upriver. In their conference near Morvin's Landing, Morgan changed his mind. He needed Johnson to come with him. The Texan was crestfallen over the decision, but he had no other choice. The boats he needed were either burning or steaming upriver.

Hobson's division spent the night of July 7 at Bardstown Junction gathering supplies. The soldiers stayed there until late the following morning. They reached Garnettsville before dark on July 8 and encamped. Instead of continuing the march into Brandenburg, twelve miles distant, Hobson decided to rest his troops. He started his march toward the river before dawn on July 9.

The stop at Garnettsville was costly. Hobson let the best chance of catching Morgan in Kentucky slip through his fingers. Colonel August Kautz called Hobson's failure to make a night attack at Brandenburg "the most serious error committed" in the pursuit. Adam Johnson admitted the great danger that Morgan's Division had faced: "If there had been any consuming desire on the part of the Federals to capture us, no better opportunity ever presented

A photograph of officers of the Tenth Kentucky Cavalry in the field. Captain Henry Clay Meriwether stands in the top row, second from the left. Note that some officers wore no uniforms, which allowed them to blend in well with the civilian population. *From Adam Johnson's* Partisan Rangers *of the Confederate States Army (1904).*

itself than occurred during the crossing at Brandenburg...Had they closely followed us and attacked vigorously our divided force while crossing, it must have proven disastrous to us."

As the last of Morgan's men rode up the river hill, Hobson's advance pickets galloped into Brandenburg. The Union scouts caught sight of the Rebels, who laughed and waved at them from across the river. The Federals took a few shots at the raiders before they rode away. Hobson could not believe his eyes. Morgan's raiders were loose in the North!

Chapter 3

Into the "Promised Land"

The raiders broke camp at dawn on July 9 and headed north to Corydon. The sweet smells of the summer air refreshed them, and the beautiful farms along their route reminded them of better times. Morgan's troopers must have felt like they had just entered the "Promised Land." The hard hand of war had not touched Indiana like it had done in Kentucky and Tennessee. Farm fields grew thick with corn, wheat and oats. Chicken coops offered fresh meat and eggs. Barns were filled with fodder. Cupboards held an abundance of cakes, pies, jams, breads, cheeses, butter and milk. Best of all, the farmers owned plenty of horses. Unfortunately, the raiders would soon discover that the horses in Indiana and Ohio were not meant for use in the cavalry. Most of the horses on Northern farms were bred for working the land and hauling goods to market. They were not trained to handle the fast long-distance rides that the cavalrymen of both sides would demand from them.

Over the course of the previous day, Colonel Lewis Jordan of the Indiana militia had supervised citizens and militiamen in the creation of a temporary breastwork of fence rails and logs along a low ridge located one mile south of Corydon. The fortification covered almost a mile-long front from the New Amsterdam Road on the west to the Laconia Road on the east. Unfortunately, the barricades on the Mauckport and Laconia roads were laid off too far north; a rise fifty yards in front of the works would shelter the enemy until it reached that distance from the Union line.

Colonel Jordan placed his Sixth Indiana Legion companies behind the temporary breastworks alongside the citizen volunteers. His total force,

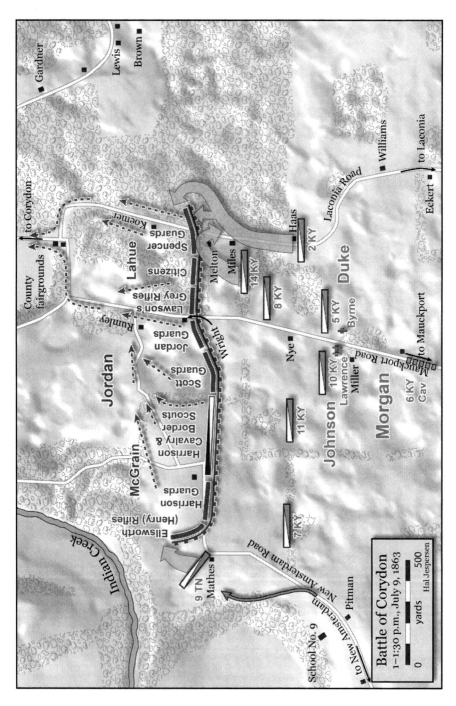

Map of the Battle of Corydon, Indiana. *Author's collection.*

composed of mainly Harrison County volunteers, amounted to about 450 men. Most were armed with nothing more than old muskets and squirrel guns, and they were dressed in plain clothes. Captain George W. Lahue commanded the left flank, with his Spencer Guards anchoring that end of the Union line. Major Thomas McGrain Jr., commanding the right flank, placed his own company, the Ellsworth Rifles, on a hill from which the whole battlefield could be viewed. The Ellsworth Rifles were armed with Henry repeating rifles (hence, the company's nickname, "Henry Rifles"). These guns would prove valuable in the coming fight.

As the hot, humid day approached 1:00 p.m., Captain Hines's advance guard of the Fourteenth Kentucky unexpectedly ran into Lahue's Spencer Guards on the Laconia Road. Lahue's men fired a volley that killed and wounded twelve of the Kentuckians, including Colonel Richard Morgan's acting adjutant, Lieutenant Spencer Thorpe, who received a bullet in the shoulder. The raiders fell back to the woods while Colonel Morgan called for reinforcements. Colonel Johnson, whose brigade marched at the head of the main column, deployed his regiments to the left and right of the Mauckport Road, while Colonel Duke placed his brigade in support. Johnson's cavalrymen dismounted, and his whole line opened fire from long distance. He then ordered the Seventh Kentucky Cavalry to charge the Union right flank, but the storm of lead from McGrain's Henry repeaters repulsed the attack. "The fighting was very sharp for the space of 20 minutes in that quarter," remembered one of Jordan's volunteers.

Realizing that a frontal assault might fail, Johnson dismounted the Ninth Tennessee Cavalry on the left flank and the Second Kentucky Cavalry on the right. Other units joined them. "In an instant the line was dismounted, and forwarding quickly into a line of battle, charged them with a yell and with great determination," wrote Lieutenant Kelion Peddicord of the Fourteenth Kentucky. As the regiments advanced simultaneously, Lawrence's Parrotts and one of Byrne's howitzers lobbed shot and shell into the enemy line. "The shells sang the ugly kind of music over our heads," recalled militiaman Simeon K. Wolfe, who was a newspaper editor and a state senator. The militia's piles of fence rails offered little protection from the projectiles, and soon the untried home guards and armed citizens lost their composure. "A few hundred of these featherbed soldiers fled at the first fire," remembered Private Thomas Berry of the Fourteenth Kentucky. Their withdrawal quickly became a rout.

"From this time the fight was converted into a series of skirmishes," wrote Wolfe. "Each man seemed to fight upon his own hook, mostly after the manner of bushwhackers." Jordan's men crowded the only road leading to the rear and into Corydon. When they saw a portion of the Fourteenth Kentucky had cut off the plank road to Louisville, the major escape route out of Corydon, the militiamen panicked. Byrne advanced an artillery piece to a hill overlooking the town's fairgrounds. He saw a great opportunity to force the retreating home guards into submission. Byrne shelled the town, causing little damage other than convincing Colonel Jordan to surrender his infantry. Most of Jordan's mounted units managed to find a way out. In less than thirty minutes, the Battle of Corydon was over.

The Confederates lost 8 killed and 33 wounded. Three militiamen were killed and 2 were wounded, 1 fatally. Morgan captured and paroled 345 of Jordan's force. Sixteen-year-old schoolgirl Attia Porter from Corydon mused over the battle, "Now that all the danger is over, it is real funny to think how our men did run...It made Morgan so mad to think a few home guards dared to fight his men. I am glad they done it just to spite him...I think that was the awfullest [sic] day I ever passed in my life."

While Morgan took a nap at the Kintner Hotel, his men sacked the stores and relieved the citizens of their valuables, food and horses. The officers tended to look the other way when it came to these activities. They were in the land of their enemy now. The people of the North would at last feel the sting of war that citizens of the South had endured for two years. A Corydon newspaper described the looting by Morgan's Division:

> *In the mean time his men commenced pillaging the stores…and they took what they pleased without let or hindrance. Mr. Denbo was sent for by Captain Charlton Morgan, the General's brother, and compelled to open his store. Every thing in the shape of ready-made clothing, hats, caps, boots, shoes, etc., was taken, Captain Morgan taking a piece of fine gray cassimere, out of which to make a suit for "John." For all of these goods, amounting in value to about $3,500, Mr. Denbo received the sum of $140 in Confederate scrip, some of which was dated as late as May, 1863…Upon each of the three flouring-mills in Corydon a levy was made of $1,000, to be paid in consideration of Morgan's refraining to burn them. The chivalry, however, graciously condescended to receive 2,100 in greenbacks in liquidation of their claim upon the mill property…They entered private houses with impunity, ate all the victual the ladies had cooked for the Home Guards, and compelled them to cook more.*

At Corydon, General Morgan first heard the terrible news about the Confederate army's surrender at Vicksburg and General Robert E. Lee's defeat at Gettysburg. Any hope that Morgan had of meeting up with Lee in Pennsylvania had vanished. However, that would not stop Morgan from executing his raid. His men spent the night in Palmyra, Indiana.

General Hobson and his officers unanimously decided to pursue the raiders into Indiana, even though his orders from Burnside did not explicitly say to do so. Waiting for orders from Boyle or Burnside might delay them even more at a time when every hour counted. Throughout the day on July 9, steamboats ferried Hobson's force across the Ohio River. By morning, all of its troopers, horses and equipment were on Hoosier soil. The men were much more anxious to catch Morgan now that he had set foot in a Northern state. They struck after Morgan's trail with the will and determination to bring the guerrilla chief to bay, once and for all.

Governor Oliver P. Morton was appalled by Morgan's invasion of Indiana. He declared a state of emergency and called out the militia. Hoosiers were not the only ones alarmed by Morgan's presence. Citizens from all over the lower Midwest were convinced that Morgan and his "terrible men" were headed their way. "Lightning" Ellsworth tapped out misleading telegrams indicating that Morgan had four thousand—no, make that twelve thousand—men in Indiana. Soon, Ellsworth had many people believing a full-scale invasion of Indiana had begun. Northern newspapers labeling the invaders as "bloodthirsty cutthroats," "murderers" and "thieves" helped to increase the widespread delirium ahead of Morgan's column.

General Burnside suffered from disbelief, too. Morgan had outwitted him and his subordinates. It was time to take decisive action. Burnside contacted his subordinate commander of the District of Indiana, Brigadier General Orlando B. Willcox, to do just that. Burnside instructed Willcox to prepare a defense for Indianapolis in case of attack from Morgan. Willcox would also direct all of the Indiana troops to be used to halt Morgan or drive him from the state. A West Point graduate and veteran of First Manassas, Willcox seemed the right man for the job, but the task of stopping the raiders before they could escape to Kentucky or enter Ohio would prove to be a more difficult task than he expected.

The citizens of Indiana responded enthusiastically to the call from the governor. Men from little towns and villages throughout the Hoosier State left their shops and stores to join their local home guard unit. The farmers, fresh from their fields, did the same. Some donned their militia uniforms; most came in the clothes they normally wore. They brought their squirrel guns, flintlocks, shotguns and hunting rifles. They were determined to defend their native soil from the Rebel horde, no matter the cost.

Union brigadier general Orlando B. Willcox commanded the District of Indiana during Morgan's Raid. He led a division in the IX Corps and then served in the U.S. Army in the West until 1887. He was awarded the Medal of Honor in 1895 for gallantry at the Battle of First Manassas. *Courtesy of U.S. Army HEC, MOLLUS Collection.*

On July 10, Morgan led his division north from Palmyra to Salem, where its two hundred home guards were dispersed without firing a shot. Morgan's men cleaned out the town's stores, taking goods to satisfy their needs and desires. Boots, shoes, saddles, harnesses and horses possessed military value, but ladies' garments, calico, silk, bird cages and ice skates were nothing more than worthless keepsakes the raiders would discard over time. They also stole whiskey from Salem's saloons for use on the long, hot, dusty trail ahead. The looting was prevalent, but Morgan indulged his men. The road ahead was uncertain and dangerous for them.

About 2:00 p.m., as the raiders left Salem, they put the Louisville, New Albany & Chicago Railroad depot and bridges to the torch. While they marched toward Vienna, Morgan sent a detachment to Seymour to destroy tracks and bridges of the Ohio & Mississippi Railroad. The raiders rode into the railroad town of Vienna late that afternoon. It, too, shared Salem's fate. Taking the road east, the division camped for the night at Lexington. Although Willcox had trouble locating Morgan's exact position, Hobson's Provisional Division made good progress; it reached Salem that evening, seven hours after the raiders had left town.

The Confederate column rode north at dawn and passed through Paris. To prevent an enemy force from getting in his path, Morgan sent a squad toward Madison to feint an attack on that city. It worked well. When the alarm was raised, Madison's militia stayed to protect their homes, leaving the Confederates' course clear. Along their route to Vernon, Morgan's men foraged for food and drink from the houses, took supplies from the stores and shops and exchanged broken-down horses for fresh ones. Under an intense

July sun, the raiders averaged twenty-one hours a day in the saddle and forty miles between camps. The best horses would collapse after about twenty miles of continuous riding, but the inferior workhorses would go lame sooner. As a result, Morgan's Division left a trail of half-dead or disabled horses in its wake. This placed Hobson's men at a disadvantage, since they, too, needed to replace their own horses with civilians' horses in order to keep up with the Confederates' incredible pace. Consequently, Hoosiers living along the raid path were displeased with the soldiers of both sides.

As the Rebel column approached Vernon about 4:00 p.m., Morgan's scouts discovered over one thousand militiamen and regular Union troops with artillery ensconced on the Muscatatuck River bluffs south of town. Morgan sent two successive flags of truce to the Union commanders, Colonel Hugh T. Williams and Brigadier General John Love, to demand the surrender of their forces. Both demands were refused, but then Love called for Morgan's surrender. Morgan was annoyed, but knowing that the Union pursuit had gained ground on him, he could not afford to fight these men. Morgan backed away and rode southeast to Dupont, where his men set up camp about 11:00 p.m. The stalemate at Vernon had cost Morgan valuable time. Hobson reached Lexington that same evening. Dupont stood only seventeen miles northeast of Lexington—a good half-day's ride. Morgan failed to realize that by retreating to Dupont, he had shortened the distance between himself and Hobson.

Morgan's troopers left Dupont at 3:00 a.m. on Sunday, July 12, after a productive night of destroying the tracks, bridges and warehouses of the Madison & Indianapolis Railroad. Morgan's column proceeded northeast through Bryantsburg to Versailles. Hams dangled from the saddles of the raiders who had grabbed them from Mayfield's pork house in Dupont. At Versailles, the Confederate general received the surrender of Colonel James Cravens and his three hundred home guards without a shot being fired. The raiders did not linger long. After confiscating horses and provisions, they turned northeast, passing through Pierceville, Milan and Clinton. Their tiring day in the saddle ended at the Ferris Schoolhouse, two miles south of Sunman, while Hobson made camp near Versailles. Morgan decided to allot his boys a couple more hours rest. With Cincinnati, the seventh-largest city in the United States, being so near, the road ahead would require all the men could give.

Amazingly, a troop train loaded with 2,500 militiamen under Colonel James Gavin sat all night on a sidetrack at Sunman. Their overall commander was Major General Lew Wallace, the future New Mexico territorial governor

Major General Lewis Wallace led the Indiana militia during Morgan's Great Raid. In 1864, he commanded Union forces at Monocacy, the "Battle that saved Washington, D.C." Wallace authored the classic 1880 novel *Ben Hur: A Tale of Christ. Courtesy of the Library of Congress.*

destined to author the epic novel *Ben Hur* and capture the outlaw Billy the Kid. In September 1862, Wallace had successfully defended Cincinnati from Major General Kirby Smith's incursion into northern Kentucky. At this moment in history, however, the Indiana general seemed unaware that his adversary's whole division was camped two miles from his men. As Gavin's soldiers chugged toward Lawrenceburg early the next morning, their train crossed Morgan's path only minutes before his advance guard reached the tracks.

On the night of July 14, Colonel Gavin's 104th Indiana Militia would be involved in a horrific friendly fire incident at Hardinsburgh. Gavin's nervous volunteers, inhibited by the darkness, mistook Colonel Kline G. Shyrock's 105th Indiana Militia for Morgan's raiders. The regiments exchanged gunfire. Before their error was realized, seven men lay dead and twenty were wounded.

When Burnside received confirmation that Morgan had turned northeast from Versailles, the Union commander correctly concluded that the Rebel general planned to enter Ohio. Early on the afternoon of July 12, Burnside sent a telegram to Ohio's governor David Tod requesting that militia be sent for Cincinnati's defense. Soon afterward, with Governor Tod's consent, Burnside declared martial law on the city, and the governor, in turn, called out the Ohio militia. War had arrived again on the doorstep of the Buckeye State.

Chapter 4

"The Darkest of All Nights"

Reveille sounded in Morgan's camp before dawn on July 13, 1863. As the weary raiders slowly climbed onto their horses, none of the men could say they had enjoyed a good night's rest. Living on four hours' sleep a day was starting to take its toll on their health. Casualties from fighting and straggling had slowly pecked away at the division. About 2,000 of the original 2,460 troopers were present this day. Only the raiders' youthful strength, sheer determination and sense that they were accomplishing something extraordinary would get them through the many miles ahead. Little did they know that this day would be special for them. The next thirty-six hours would be one of the American military's greatest achievements in endurance.

Moving eastward, the Confederates went to their normal business of marching long distances, destroying railroads, fighting off local militia and foraging from civilians. The raiders began their day tearing up tracks and burning trestles on the Indianapolis, Lawrenceburg & Cincinnati Railroad. Then they passed through Hubbell's Corner, New Alsace, Dover and Logan's Crossroads before reaching West Harrison, Indiana, which sits astride the Indiana-Ohio border eighteen miles east of the Ferris Schoolhouse. Morgan looked over his shoulder. In the distance, he could plainly see a large dust cloud following them. It was Hobson's cavalry. The bluecoats trailed by only five hours.

Morgan's incessant marching and countermarching for twenty hours per day, combined with George Ellsworth's false messages to Willcox and his officers, had allowed Morgan to traverse 186 miles of Hoosier land with little cost to his division. As the Confederate advance guard galloped over the Whitewater River covered bridge into Harrison, the first Buckeye town the raiders would visit, one could almost hear the people of Indiana breathe a sigh of relief. They were glad to see Morgan go, and good riddance to him! Morgan returned the sentiment. He was equally happy to leave behind a state whose citizens had flocked to defend their homes well beyond his expectations. Nearly sixty-five thousand regulars, home guards and militiamen had mobilized to stop Morgan in Indiana.

The Buckeyes' defense of their state would prove to be stiffer. Governor Tod's call to the militia had met with overwhelming success. When Morgan's men reached Harrison at noon, nearly ten thousand regulars and citizen-soldiers had gathered in downtown Cincinnati and the nearby city of Hamilton. Cincinnati was one of the Union's largest producers of military equipment, supplies, weapons, wagons and steamboats. Burnside would defend the city at all costs. Only twenty miles of road separated Morgan from Burnside's Cincinnati headquarters. It seemed as if the two generals would meet in a showdown.

But a showdown was not meant to be. Morgan intended to attack neither Cincinnati nor Hamilton. He had read in local newspapers that Burnside had already declared martial law. Learning from his experience in Indiana, Morgan could only assume that these cities were teeming with troops waiting to get their hands on him. Besides, an assault on either city would waste valuable time, and his men could lose themselves among the labyrinth of streets. An attack on a well-defended town could easily turn into a replay of the Lebanon battle.

Like many times before, Morgan planned to trick his adversary into thinking he was planning an attack on one of the two Union strongholds. From Harrison, he would send large detachments toward Cincinnati and Hamilton. Before these detachments came too close, they would veer away and return to the main column as it passed between the two cities. Morgan planned to "thread the needle," so to speak.

However, he had another major obstacle to contend with. The Cincinnati, Hamilton & Dayton (CH&D) Railroad connected the cities, which were only twenty miles apart. Burnside could easily take advantage of this railway by transporting large numbers of troops to various stations to block Morgan's path. Scouts had warned Morgan in June about this railroad. The CH&D Railroad would be Morgan's greatest obstacle in passing around Cincinnati.

To neutralize the dangers of the railroad and the large numbers of troops in the region, Morgan decided to perform a night march. At Harrison's

American House Hotel, he briefed Johnson and Duke about the plan. A night march through a complicated grid of suburban roads was a bold and risky move, but it had to be done. Camping anywhere near Cincinnati could be even riskier.

The raiders refreshed themselves at Harrison before the long journey ahead. They gathered food from the residents, broke into the town's stores for supplies and took horses wherever they could be found. Of course, with Ohio being one of the Confederacy's severest enemies, the raiders' looting seemed to only increase. Colonel Basil Duke wrote that his men "pillaged like boys robbing an orchard. I would not have believed that such a passion could have been developed so ludicrously, among any body of civilized men. They would (with few exceptions) throw away their plunder after awhile, like children, tired of their toys." Churches were off limits to pilfering. Private dwellings could not be entered except when they were unoccupied or when the owners invited them in. "Where people stayed at home and behaved themselves, we did not disturb the house," explained Private Curtis Burke, "but where people run away from home, we rated them as home guards or bushwhackers, and took everything in the way of something to eat in the house."

Before leaving, Colonel Johnson summoned Captain Sam Burk Taylor and his cousin, Lieutenant John W. McLean, who were both from the Tenth Kentucky Cavalry. Both men had spent time before the war in the Cincinnati area, so they were well acquainted with the streets and markets where troops would likely gather. Johnson informed the men of their special mission. They would ride down the Harrison Turnpike into downtown Cincinnati and gather intelligence about the strength and readiness of Burnside's forces. Especially important to learn was the viability that these troops could march out and block Morgan somewhere in the suburbs. Taylor and McLean, dressed in their farm clothes, trotted away.

Morgan divided his troops. One group of 500 men headed for Miamitown, while Morgan would lead the other 1,500 men, with the artillery and wagon train, toward New Haven. The wheels for the greatest cavalry march in American history were set into motion. As the rear guard departed Harrison, the raiders burned the beautiful covered bridge over the Whitewater River. Within an hour, Hobson's troopers reached the smoldering remains. The loss of this bridge cost them several hours as they sought to find a ford for the artillery. Hobson spent the night in the same Harrison hotel that Morgan had occupied during the day, while his troopers tumbled from their horses into the streets fast asleep.

Confederate captain Samuel B. Taylor, a nephew of President Zachary Taylor, served with the Tenth Kentucky Cavalry. Samuel helped capture steamboats at Brandenburg, Kentucky, and scouted deep into Cincinnati. Morgan often picked him to execute dangerous missions. *Courtesy of Cowan's Auctions Inc., Cincinnati, Ohio.*

As the sun set over southwest Ohio, Morgan's troopers lit their path with the flames from the New Baltimore Bridge over the Great Miami River. They heard the distant sounds of musketry at Miamitown Bridge, where Morgan's flankers brushed aside home guards led by a Cincinnati police detective, Major Bill Raney. By nightfall, Morgan's column had passed through Bevis. The detachment sent toward Cincinnati rendezvoused with them there, as did Captain Taylor and Lieutenant McClain, who reported to Johnson that the city was full of enemy troops, but the military situation appeared chaotic. No concerted Union advance would occur on this night, they believed.

General Burnside and his staff were frenetic. They worked tirelessly throughout the night to determine Morgan's position. The telegraph at headquarters buzzed with constant activity. Ellsworth sent errant messages from Harrison's telegraph office to confuse the Union high command. One message said Morgan was spotted near Hamilton; another indicated Cincinnati. Suddenly, Morgan showed up at New Baltimore and Bevis. It seemed the raider was everywhere all at once.

Burnside's subordinates in the city were quite capable of dealing with Morgan. The District of Ohio commander, Brigadier General Jacob Dolson Cox, was a staunch abolitionist Ohio senator who had earned a great reputation for his hard fighting in McClellan's 1861 West Virginia campaign and for his decisive leadership at the 1862 Battle of South Mountain, Maryland. Cox would not squelch an opportunity to deal a deathblow to the enemy. Also serving on Burnside's staff was an old West Pointer, Brigadier General Jacob Ammen, a hero of the Battle of Shiloh. He hailed from nearby Georgetown, Ohio, and therefore held a vested interest in keeping

Morgan away from his hometown. Ammen commanded the troops manning the Cincinnati defensive line.

However, no matter how skilled Burnside's officers were in Napoleonic warfare, Morgan and his officers were better than they when it came to executing guerrilla warfare. No instructors taught Morgan's style of war in the military academies. It was new to most generals—except to the veteran cavalry leaders on Morgan's tail. That's why Morgan's men feared Hobson's division more than any other.

While Burnside and his officers hatched out a plan to trap the raiders, the Confederate column plodded through the calm, moonless night. The men started to pass out from exhaustion as they closed in on Springfield (Springdale Post Office). Lieutenant Kelion Franklin Peddicord of the Fourteenth Kentucky Cavalry remembered the harrowing night ride for the rest of his life:

> It was without doubt the darkest of all nights. The troops were almost exhausted for want of sleep. Many of them during the night, while asleep, wandered off on some of the many side roads, notwithstanding the officers' vigilance to keep all awake by riding from the head of their companies to the rear and back again, and constantly urging them, if they loved their country's cause, to keep each other awake. Oftentimes I have seen on that raid both man and horse nodding together, and at such times the horse staggering like one intoxicated.

Duke had trouble guiding his men through the pitch-black night. Since Morgan had forbidden everyone except the scouts from lighting torches, to prevent the enemy from detecting their line of march, the scouts relied on ancient cavalry techniques to find their way. For example, they searched for dust trails and horse slaver droppings in the roads to point them in the right direction. The march turned into a "nightmare," Duke wrote.

The column passed through Springfield after midnight and at 2:00 a.m. approached the key to the raid around Cincinnati: the Cincinnati, Hamilton & Dayton Railroad crossing at Glendale. Had Burnside deployed troops to guard the town? Would Morgan be trapped among the thousands of bluecoats covering every direction—Hamilton to the north, Cincinnati to the south, Hobson to the west and, perhaps, Glendale to the east?

Much to Morgan's relief and surprise, not one Union soldier occupied the quiet, upscale village. In fact, one could hear a pin drop if it wasn't

Confederate lieutenant Kelion F. Peddicord was captured at Bashan, Ohio, with most of the Fourteenth Kentucky Cavalry. After the war, his sister wrote a biography of him and Morgan's raiders. *Courtesy of University of Kentucky Archives.*

for the clatter of the raiders' horse hooves on the cobblestones. Unknown to Morgan, Burnside had sent a troop train containing the Nineteenth Ohio Battery up the railway to Hamilton. The train had passed through Glendale only thirty minutes prior to the arrival of Morgan's vanguard!

Once again, Morgan's tactics of feints combined with Ellsworth's false telegrams had paid off. As the first streaks of the morning's light appeared on the horizon, Morgan felt comfortable that his plan would succeed. While celebrating over a box of cigars and a bottle of brandy at Sharonville's Twelve Mile House, Morgan and his colonels decided to spread out and forage. With the immediate danger behind them, their men needed new mounts, supplies and food. A six-mile swath through the northeastern suburbs of Cincinnati would be cleaned out of these items before the morning was through.

One flanking detachment passed through Reading, where the Sisters of Notre Dame de Namur Academy stood. The raiders went to the school to look for the nuns' horses. There were none to be found. The caretakers had hidden them in the basement. The disappointed Rebels continued on their way. Major General William T. Sherman would personally enroll his daughter Minnie in the school the following January. For now, Minnie and the rest of the Sherman children were safely sleeping in their beds at their house in Lancaster, Ohio.

John C. and Eliza Bowen Hunt were typical of civilians who suffered from Morgan's Great Raid. The Hunts lost six horses to the raiders. Only two horses were recovered; the others were partially reimbursed by the State of Ohio's Morgan Raid Claims Commission. *Courtesy of Tom and Katie Bell.*

As the main column trotted through East Sycamore, General Morgan took a breakfast break at the home of a wealthy farmer, John Schenck. When Morgan arrived in the yard, his scouts warned him that there was a child with smallpox lying bedridden in the parlor. The windows were shuttered, and the doors were covered with white sheets, standard Victorian ways of saying, "Keep Out!" Nevertheless, the fine ladies of the Schenck family served the general and his staff breakfast out on the porch. All the while, a family of escaped slaves and Schenck's two expensive horses remained hidden in the straw-covered parlor. Morgan and his men never noticed them. Their minds were focused on the huge Camp Dennison to the east.

Camp Dennison, named after Governor Tod's predecessor, was a seven-hundred-acre training and mustering facility hosting one of the North's largest military hospitals. In April 1861, Major General George McClellan had established the camp, and then-colonel William S. Rosecrans had laid it out. It was an impressive place—an inviting prize for someone like Morgan. The confident Confederate general would try his luck at capturing it.

The commander of Camp Dennison at the time of Morgan's Raid was thirty-year-old Lieutenant Colonel George W. Neff. A native of Cincinnati, George knew the roads and terrain surrounding the camp very well. Before the Civil War began, George had partnered with his brother in running a

Union lieutenant colonel George W. Neff successfully defended Camp Dennison during Morgan's Great Raid. He earned a promotion for his efforts, eventually attaining the rank of brevet brigadier general. After the war, he ran a profitable insurance business. *Courtesy of U.S. Army HEC, Roger D. Hunt Collection.*

wholesale shoe business, and he had formed a militia company, composed mostly of Cincinnati firefighters, called the "Rover Guards." In 1861, Neff helped recruit Union volunteers for the Second Kentucky (U.S.) Infantry and was commissioned as the regiment's lieutenant colonel. At the Battle of Scary Creek, (West) Virginia, he was captured and sent to Libby Prison in Richmond, Virginia. He was exchanged on September 30, 1862, ending fourteen months of incarceration. Neff returned home on leave of absence, and on January 15, 1863, he accepted the appointment as commander of Camp Dennison.

On the afternoon of July 12, Lieutenant Colonel Neff received word that Morgan's Division had ridden into southeast Indiana and had turned east toward Cincinnati. Neff had only about six hundred regular soldiers—most of them new recruits and convalescents—and only enough guns to arm about four hundred of them. However, recognizing the strategic importance of the camp, Neff resolved to defend it at all costs. At 10:00 p.m., he ordered his mounted pickets from Companies E, F, G and H of the Eleventh Ohio Cavalry to move out at a distance of four to six miles to patrol all of the main roads leading to the camp.

At 4:00 a.m. on July 13, Neff sent Captain William Von Doehn, assistant adjutant general, and Captain Joseph L. Proctor, Eighteenth U.S. Infantry, with a detachment of 50 able-bodied men to dig rifle pits on a steep hill overlooking the intersection of three major regional roads: Kugler Mill Road, Loveland Road and the Madisonville Turnpike. Because an enemy approaching from the west would be compelled to march on one of the three roads, Lieutenant Colonel Neff understood the necessity of defending this position. At 3:00 p.m., he dispatched Captain Proctor and 150 convalescent infantrymen to the entrenchments with orders to hold them if Morgan attacked. To protect the northern and eastern approaches to the camp, Neff posted pickets at all the Little Miami River bridges between Milford and Fort Ancient. He also placed a heavy guard on the Madisonville Pike and positioned troops in ambush along the hill southwest of camp, in case Morgan penetrated the rifle pits.

Throughout the day and into the night, reinforcements arrived by train, and by five o'clock the next morning, Neff would add 1,400 raw militiamen to his ranks. However, he had no arms or ammunition to give them. The weapons he had requested from General Burnside were still in Cincinnati.

At 1:30 a.m. on July 14, Brigadier General Jacob D. Cox warned Neff of Morgan's appearance near Glendale. "Let us know what you can learn of the route between you and us," Cox wrote in his telegram. "The camp must be held!" Three hours later, a citizen brought word that the Confederates had been spotted only five miles distant from the camp. Lieutenant Colonel Neff immediately sent fifty more armed convalescents to the rifle pits, and he directed one hundred militiamen with axes to fell trees across the roads and in front of the earthworks. No sooner had this been accomplished than, just after 6:00 a.m., the lead elements of Morgan's column appeared at the barricade on the Kugler Mill Road opposite the entrenchments. Captain Proctor gave the signal to fire. His Union defenders let loose a terrific volley that sent the Confederate cavalrymen reeling.

General Morgan ordered Colonel Adam Johnson's men to dismount and fan out along the hillside west of the crossroads. Slowly advancing to the *abatis* along Sycamore Creek, the Confederate skirmishers commenced a brisk firefight with the convalescents and militia. When Morgan realized the Union troops would not budge from their rifle pits, he brought up a section of Byrne's Battery, which unlimbered on the crest of the hill behind the cavalry. The howitzers shelled Proctor's position for almost half an hour, but the Union lines held firm.

Johnson's skirmishers were unable to dislodge the enemy from their earthworks. To avoid a time-consuming engagement, Morgan chose to withdraw. No casualties were reported on either side. The felled tree obstructions forced the Confederates to backtrack to Montgomery, where they reunited with Duke's First Brigade. From there, the raiders headed east to ford the Little Miami River at Porter's Mill.

The scouts from the Fourteenth Kentucky placed a barrier among the rails of the nearby Little Miami Railroad to prevent troop trains from sneaking

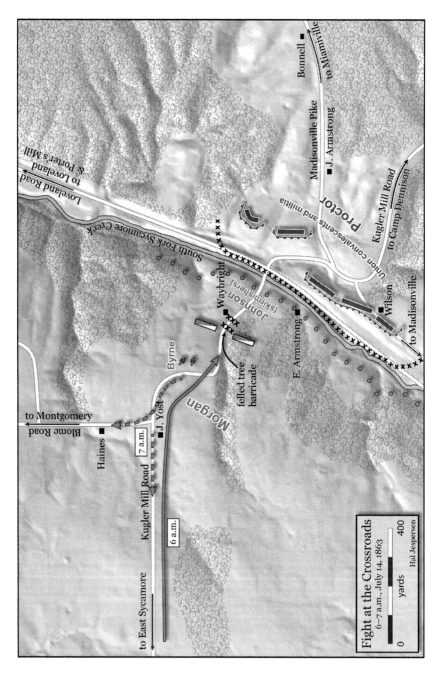

Map of the fight at the crossroads three miles west of Camp Dennison, Ohio. *Author's collection.*

up on the column as it rode over the tracks. A train suddenly appeared from the north. When it passed by, the raiders fired into it, causing the engineer to put on more steam. He failed to notice the barrier around the bend. The locomotive Kilgore struck the barrier, leaped the tracks and tumbled over the embankment, killing the fireman and severely wounding the engineer. "There lay the monster floundering in the field like a fish out of water, with nothing but the tender attached," recalled Peddicord. Miraculously, the passenger cars filled with 115 raw militiamen cruised to a stop on the tracks. Morgan's men captured the greenhorns without a shot and marched them to General Morgan, who, after paroling them, told the recruits they could walk the rest of the way to Camp Dennison.

Just before 7:30 a.m. on July 14, Morgan's scouts rode south from Porter's Mill Ford on the Glendale–Milford Road. They surprised eight of Captain William Von Doehn's mounted pickets, who were found playing cards on the Madisonville Turnpike Bridge over the Little Miami River. All of them were newly trained men from Captain Jacob S. Shuman's Company H, Eleventh Ohio Cavalry. The Kentuckians charged the panic-stricken Ohioans and scattered them, capturing one Union cavalryman and eight horses. The Confederates quickly pushed on toward Miamiville and the coveted Little Miami Railroad Bridge. When they reached the north end of the bridge, another detachment of Company H waited at the south end. This time, the Union pickets stood ready, and the skirmishing began in earnest.

Lieutenant Colonel Neff quickly responded to the threat by dispatching Lieutenant William H.H. Smith, Twenty-first Ohio Battery Light Artillery, with Captain Guest's two hundred militiamen of the Miami Volunteers. Only minutes earlier, Captain Guest and his infantry had arrived at the camp by rail from Cincinnati with a supply of guns and ammunition. After filing off the train, the militiamen gathered up their muskets and cartridges as quickly as they could be thrown from the boxcars, and Lieutenant Smith force-marched Guest's infantrymen up the Glendale–Milford Road to the railroad bridge. As they traversed the mile from the Camp Dennison depot, Smith had the soldiers load their weapons on the run.

Neff's reinforcements came in the nick of time. Colonel Basil Duke had bolstered the Fourteenth Kentucky scouts' skirmish line with men from the Second, Fifth and Sixth Kentucky Cavalry regiments. A detachment turned the Union right flank with a foray over the river from the mouth of a nearby creek. The raiders charged into the open woods that bordered the west line of Fletcher's farm. They soon overran Von Doehn's position,

A lithograph of the Little Miami Railroad Bridge at Miamiville, Ohio. This view faces westward. The two men are standing on Fletcher's farm lane at the position of the Miami Volunteers in the skirmish of July 14, 1863. *From Edward Mansfield's* The Ohio Railroad Guide, Illustrated *(1854).*

wounding or capturing five Eleventh Ohio cavalrymen and forcing the rest to retreat. Duke's men were preparing to set fire to the railroad bridge when Lieutenant Smith and Captain Guest's Miami Volunteers unexpectedly appeared on the scene. The militiamen charged in column and opened fire, causing the startled Confederates to fall back. Smith's men advanced to the river and retook possession of the south end of the railroad bridge. Foiled in their attempt to destroy the bridge, Morgan's troopers withdrew to the safety of the trees lining the northern river bluff.

At this moment, Lieutenant Smith assumed command of the Union forces on the field. He rallied the remaining Eleventh Ohio cavalrymen and formed them into line with Guest's infantry along the southern riverbank. Smith placed the center of the line at the railroad bridge and the Glendale–Milford Road ford. Most of the Union soldiers sought cover behind trees, bushes and the split rail fence of Fletcher's farm lane.

The skirmish evolved into a sporadic long-range firefight. The inexperienced and ill-equipped militiamen stubbornly held their line against Duke's veteran cavalrymen. General Morgan heard the firing from his headquarters at a farmhouse on the Branch Hill–Miamiville Road. He persuaded the farmer, Jacob H. Thompson, to lead him to Miamiville by the most direct route.

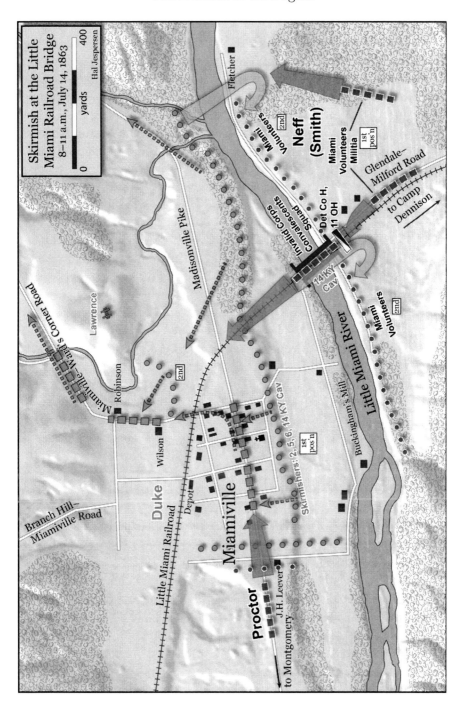

Map of the skirmish at the Little Miami Railroad Bridge near Miamiville, Ohio.
Author's collection.

They soon reached the hill above town, from which Morgan could see the vast camp laid before him. After reviewing the situation with Colonel Duke, the general ordered Lieutenant Lawrence to unlimber his section of artillery on a hill behind the center of the line. Lawrence's Parrotts fired a few rounds in the direction of the militia, and then they lobbed shells amid the Soldiers' Barracks on the north side of Camp Dennison, one mile distant. However, the barrage proved ineffective, and the militia stood their ground. Leaving the supervision of the skirmish in Duke's capable hands, Morgan galloped back to the main column to hurry them up.

About 10:30 a.m., Lieutenant Colonel Neff arrived at the railroad bridge with a squad of twenty convalescents from the Invalid Corps. The sight of reinforcements boosted the militia's morale. Minutes later, Captain Joseph L. Proctor's Union infantrymen made their timely appearance at the Madisonville Pike Bridge.

Flush with victory from his defense of the crossroads three miles west of the camp, Proctor had dispatched a large portion of his convalescent soldiers to follow Morgan's main column as it retreated to Montgomery. Proctor led the bulk of his exhausted infantrymen at the double-quick toward the sound of the guns. His skirmishers engaged the Confederate pickets on the Madisonville Turnpike, and about 10:30 a.m., Proctor's Federals captured the bridge. They quickly deployed into line of battle and opened fire on Duke's rear guard. By this time, Colonel Duke realized the skirmish had become more serious. He ordered his rear guard to evacuate Miamiville and head for the rendezvous point at Ward's Corner.

When Neff heard the crescendo of gunshots off to his left, he saw an opportunity to make his move. He called on his convalescent veterans to rise and fix bayonets, and in a stirring moment, Neff led them in a charge across the railroad bridge. The Confederate defenders fired a volley, killing one Union soldier, and then broke for the rear. A rout ensued when Neff's convalescent squad fell on the Confederates as they tried to jump into their saddles. Several Confederates were bayoneted, and others were captured, including Lieutenant Charles H. Powell of Company F, Sixth Kentucky Cavalry, who was found pinned underneath his horse. Two members of Quirk's Scouts were also among those taken prisoner.

Duke's rear guard at the Robinson farm held off Proctor's and Smith's bluecoats long enough to buy time for Duke to extract his cavalrymen from Miamiville. After regrouping, the men and artillery of the First Brigade retreated in an orderly manner northward to Ward's Corner. Their swift horses allowed the Confederates to put a safe distance between them and the

Union foot soldiers. Because Von Doehn's cavalry was too worn out, Neff was powerless to pursue the fleeing raiders.

By 11:00 a.m., the fight for the bridge was over. Duke had lost six men killed, four wounded and seven captured. Neff's casualties amounted to one man killed, several wounded, four captured and one missing. Neff immediately sent Burnside a telegram stating, "I have succeeded in saving the railroad bridge over [Little] Miami River, at Miamiville." Six days later, George Neff would receive a promotion to colonel for his successful defense of Camp Dennison. He wrote in his official after-action report, "I cannot say too much in the praise of the officers and men of this camp, and also the militia. They behaved as true men and brave soldiers. By their promptness in obeying all orders and gallant conduct, the finest camp in the United States was saved from the firebrand of the enemy."

By 9:00 a.m., all of Morgan's cavalrymen and wagons had forded the Little Miami River, which ran at a trickle because of the dry Ohio summer. The fight at Camp Dennison had done its part in keeping Neff at bay until the fording was completed. Except for an annoying squad of Loveland militiamen who sniped at Johnson's rear guard, the raiders rode unmolested to Mulberry, near which they discovered a small Union supply depot named Camp Shady. Here, Neff had been forced to leave behind fifty brand-new supply wagons and a drove of horses and mules. The raiders were thrilled by the sight. After they rummaged through the wagons and exchanged their tired horses with those from Neff's pool, they burned the vehicles and their contents.

After passing through Boston and sending flankers through Batavia, the gray, dusty column trudged into the town of Williamsburg about 4:00 p.m. on July 14. Morgan ordered the men to set up camp. They willingly obliged. At a cost of fewer than sixty men, the division had circumvented the North's largest populated area west of the Appalachian Mountains. Not only that, but the raiders had also covered eighty-five miles in thirty-five hours—the longest nonstop march of a mounted infantry division in American history. The feat would never be matched. General Morgan smiled to himself that night in Williamsburg's Kain House Hotel. He had overcome his third great obstacle of the raid. Only one more challenge remained: to recross the Ohio River!

Chapter 5

"One Continual Fight"

A 3:00 a.m. reveille woke the raiders from their deep sleep. It had been the longest rest they had received for nearly a week. Morale was high as they rode east. They knew the end of the raid was near. They just needed to find a way back to the south side of their ever-present foe, the Ohio River.

General Morgan sent a large detachment of troopers commanded by his brother, Colonel Richard Morgan, on a wide detour toward the river to scout out possible fording sites. Their columns would rendezvous somewhere near Winchester, the next largest town to the east. Colonel Morgan's column entered Georgetown in the morning. Georgetown was the childhood home of Major General Ulysses S. Grant, who was celebrating his capture of Vicksburg in far-away Mississippi. Most of Georgetown's residents were firm Unionists with personal ties to Grant. Colonel Morgan had no time to think about that. Besides, his men were under strict orders to molest no innocent men, women or children. This order was obeyed without question for the entire length of the raid, with rare exception. Men would be shot on the spot if they were caught violating this rule. It was Morgan's rule, and a Southern gentleman would never break it.

After raiding Georgetown of its horses and supplies, Colonel Morgan made his way to the river town of Ripley, a famous hotbed of abolitionism and a place well known for its ford described in Harriet Beecher Stowe's world-renowned book *Uncle Tom's Cabin*. When his scouts noticed a large body of militiamen and a cannon positioned in line outside of town, Morgan wisely declined entering the place.

From the bluff nearby, Dick could see menacing-looking Union gunboats patrolling the Ohio River in either direction. Ever since the debacle at Brandenburg, Lieutenant Commander Le Roy Fitch of the Union navy had been busy deploying his armed craft of the Mississippi Squadron from Louisville, Kentucky, to Portsmouth, Ohio. The sailors had become quite efficient at destroying small boats and rafts along this stretch of the river to prevent them from being used by Morgan's troops. Fitch's fleet of gunboats steamed up the Ohio, maintaining perfect pace with Morgan's column. Wherever Morgan happened to be, Fitch seemed to be waiting for him at the river.

A graduate of the U.S. Naval Academy class of 1856, Lieutenant Commander Le Roy Fitch was twenty-seven years old at the time of the Great Raid. Following his graduation from the academy, he served with distinction under Commander Charles H. Davis. At the beginning of the Civil War, Fitch was ordered to the Pensacola Navy Yard in Florida before being sent to the New York Navy Yard for a training assignment. There he mastered the use of his favorite weapons, the twelve-pounder and twenty-four-pounder Dahlgren howitzers. In March 1862, as a lieutenant, he was transferred to the Western Flotilla, where he quickly rose through the ranks of the Mississippi Squadron. Fitch was an outstanding naval officer who fairly earned his independent leadership role in the Civil War's Western Theater. Using innovative means, he successfully protected Federal shipping from attacks by the likes of Morgan, Wheeler and Forrest. He also controlled the steady flow of supplies to Union sympathizers; participated in several Union army amphibious operations, including Fort Donelson; and patrolled waterborne supply routes on the Tennessee, Cumberland and Ohio Rivers with a fleet of shallow-draft gunboats whose creation he had supervised. As an innovator in the art of convoy, Fitch had no equal within the U.S. Navy.

Dick Morgan turned north to brief his commander. At Winchester, he told General Morgan the bad news. The road to freedom would be longer than expected. The general gathered his men at the town cemetery to tell them that they would be heading to the fords and ferries above Portsmouth, the last navigable port of the Ohio River during the summer months. Gunboats would not be able to negotiate the shallow waters above there, he thought.

Meanwhile, General Hobson spent the day of July 14 crossing the northern suburbs of Cincinnati. The citizens cheered them on, and the ladies came out in droves to supply their boys in blue with milk, home-baked breads and plenty of fried chicken. The Northern hospitality for the Union cavalrymen had been nothing but inspiring since they crossed the Ohio River into Indiana. Hoosier and Buckeye women lined the roadside by the thousands to hand out food to the

Lieutenant Commander Le Roy Fitch commanded the Union navy vessels that prevented Morgan from crossing the Ohio River. The World War II destroyer USS *Fitch* (DD-462) was christened in his honor. *Courtesy of U.S. Army HEC, MOLLUS Collection.*

men in the saddles. Military rations were discarded in favor of these delicacies that many of the soldiers had not eaten since entering the army. One Union cavalryman later described Morgan's Raid with one phrase: "Six hundred square miles of fried chicken."

On the night of July 14, Hobson's troopers camped near Mulberry, where they were reinforced by Union raider Colonel William P. Sanders and his Michigan cavalry brigade from Danville, Kentucky. Sanders had replaced Colonel James David as the brigade commander following David's poor performance at Lebanon.

William Price "Doc" Sanders was a month short of his thirtieth birthday when he took command of the Michigan cavalry brigade. Sanders was born near Frankfort, Kentucky, but around the age of seven his family moved to Natchez, Mississippi, where he grew up in a wealthy neighborhood. His father's deep political connections allowed William to receive an appointment to West Point. William would have flunked out of his first year had it not been for the recommendation of his cousin Jefferson Davis to keep him in the academy. Sanders graduated from West Point in 1856 and was given the commission of brevet second lieutenant in the First U.S. Dragoons. He served with distinction in the Utah territory with the Second U.S. Dragoons. Although he had close ties to the South, Sanders sided with the Union cause when the Civil War erupted. He stayed with the U.S. Dragoons and in May 1861 was promoted to captain of the Sixth U.S. Cavalry, with which he served valiantly during the Peninsula Campaign and the Antietam Campaign. He went on sick leave until February 1863, at which time General Ambrose

Union colonel William P. Sanders commanded a brigade of Michigan cavalrymen who played a significant role in the Battle of Buffington Island. Promoted to brigadier general, Sanders was mortally wounded at the Siege of Knoxville on November 18, 1863. *Courtesy of U.S. Army HEC, MOLLUS Collection.*

Burnside awarded him the colonelcy of the Fifth Kentucky (U.S.) Cavalry regiment in the Army of the Ohio. For the emergency at hand, Sanders was an officer Burnside could trust.

On July 15, after being temporarily misdirected by a local guide, the Provisional Division reached Sardinia by nightfall. The Union pursuit was a day's ride behind Morgan, whose division had spent the evening at Locust Grove.

To attempt to catch Morgan, who was gaining ground each day, Hobson sent Colonel August V. Kautz with a large group of handpicked men ahead of the main column. Kautz's Ohio cavalrymen were natives of the region through which they were traveling. No civilian guides were needed, since the soldiers could direct themselves. Kautz rode off on the morning of July 16 with the mission to strike Morgan's column and delay it as long as possible.

Born in 1828 in Germany, August Valentine Kautz was raised in Brown County, Ohio, and spent much of his childhood in Georgetown, where he attended the same two-room school in which future Union generals Ulysses S. Grant, Jacob Ammen and Charles W. Blair were taught. Kautz volunteered in the Mexican-American War with the First Ohio Infantry, which saw action at the Battle of Monterrey. Kautz graduated from the West Point class of 1852 and was assigned as a second lieutenant to the Fourth U.S. Infantry, which saw combat against the Indians in the Pacific Northwest. He showed much bravery

Union colonel August V. Kautz led a brigade of Ohio cavalrymen during Morgan's Raid. Promoted in April 1864, he transferred to the Eastern Theater and participated in the Wilson-Kautz Raid. After the war, he served in the U.S. Army on the western frontier until 1892. *Courtesy of U.S. Army HEC, MOLLUS Collection.*

and steadfastness in battle and was wounded twice in skirmishes with the Indians during the Rogue River Wars. A captain in the Sixth U.S. Cavalry at the beginning of the Civil War, Kautz was transferred in 1862 to the Western Theater and was made colonel of the Second Ohio Cavalry, which fought Indians on the Kansas frontier. The Second Ohio Cavalry was reassigned to the Department of the Ohio, and for a short time, Kautz commanded Camp Chase in Columbus before taking command of a brigade of cavalry.

About 1:00 p.m. on July 16, Morgan's vanguard stumbled on a roadblock at Stoney Ridge defended by a forty-man home guard unit called the Pike County Military Committee. These men refused to surrender. They opened fire on the raiders, but after a short resistance, the heavy firepower of Morgan's troopers convinced the small group to give up. The prisoners marched with the raiders to Jasper, where one of the home guards, Joseph McDougal, threw a few too many curses at his captors. When no one would step forward to guide the raiders to the ford across the Scioto River, they threatened to shoot one of the home guards. Still no one budged. Then the raiders bound the loud-mouthed McDougal, put him in a skiff and shot him dead. It was one of the rare times along the raid when the Confederates killed an unarmed man.

Before leaving Jasper, Morgan's men looted the town's stores and burned many of its barns, stables and mills as retribution for the delay at Stoney Ridge. They also set fire to canalboats and bridges of the Ohio & Erie Canal. The destruction of these bridges would delay Kautz's Buckeyes for six hours, effectively ending their attempt to catch Morgan's rear guard.

After Morgan's troopers found the ford, they crossed the Scioto River into Piketon and headed for the city of Jackson, where they encamped about 10:00 p.m. Jackson's citizen-defenders fled without resistance at the sight of the Confederate juggernaut. They were rounded up and confined to the Jackson County fairgrounds until paroled the next morning. The raiders went to work burning the railroad facilities in town and breaking open stores for supplies and plunder. Frantic citizens freely gave up their horses, goods and meals to the famished Rebels. General Morgan, who had read a scathing editorial in the *Jackson Standard* calling his troops the "scum of the South," ordered the newspaper's printing press destroyed and its typeset thrown out the window. Hobson's troopers, who would arrive in Jackson the following night, retaliated for this disgraceful act by destroying the equipment of the *Jackson Express*, which was owned by an alleged Copperhead.

Morgan continued his journey eastward, sending Colonel Johnson's Second Brigade southeast toward Vinton to look for General Judah's Union force, which, according to newspaper reports, had embarked from Cincinnati on steamboats bound for Portsmouth. Meanwhile, Morgan and Duke rode toward Wilkesville.

Defense of the nearby city of Chillicothe and the surrounding region was given to Colonel Benjamin P. Runkle, the Forty-fifth Ohio Infantry's former commander whom General Burnside and Governor Tod had ordered to report to Colonel William R. Putnam at Marietta for special duty. At Chillicothe, Runkle gathered a force of 5,300 raw militiamen and one piece of artillery "in bad condition." Only 2,300 of the men were armed. During the night of July 16, by order of General Burnside, Colonel Runkle and 1,500 untrained militiamen from Ross County embarked on a Marietta & Cincinnati Railroad train bound for Hamden, reaching there early the next morning. Runkle expected 1,000 more militiamen to join him, but they never arrived.

Runkle marched his 1,500 troops six miles south on the Hamden Road to a hamlet known as Berlin Crossroads, or Berlin. Besides being a stop on the Marietta & Cincinnati Railroad, the town boasted a large flour mill owned by Rufus Hunsinger. Runkle would make a stand here, with the goal of delaying Morgan long enough for Hobson to catch up to the raiders. Otherwise, Runkle hoped to divert the Confederates in the direction of Judah and Fitch. Runkle formed his undrilled recruits into battle lines on the heights above Berlin and placed a skirmish line from a point of woods on the Hamden Road, through the north end of the village and across the Wilkesville–Pomeroy Road. In these positions they waited anxiously for Morgan's men to appear.

The moment came about 11:00 a.m. Tom Murphy, whom his comrades nicknamed the "Wild Irishman," was one of Morgan's "goingest" scouts. As

Tom and two companions rode into Berlin Crossroads, one of Runkle's pickets called on them to halt. Tom instinctively swung his gun under the neck of his horse and took aim, but before he could get the shot off, the Union sentries fired on them. A bullet struck Murphy in the shoulder, knocking him off his horse. He was captured and carried to a nearby house to be treated. After he recovered, Union authorities transferred him to a prisoner of war camp.

Murphy's comrades galloped back to the main column to report the presence of a large Union force on the heights northeast of Berlin. General Morgan needed to know if enemy artillery stood there, but the scouts could not provide that information. About noon, Lawrence's section of artillery unlimbered on top of Keenan's Hill on the west side of Berlin. Hoping to draw counter-battery fire, the Confederate guns hurled at least five shots over the town onto Berlin Heights, creating terror among Runkle's nervous militiamen. When Runkle's pickets broke and ran pell-mell through their main line, their panic spread through the ranks uncontrollably. It took all of Runkle's energy just to prevent his whole force from stampeding. Most of the recruits fell back about two hundred yards to a place under the brow of the heights where they would be sheltered from the bombardment. Many kept running into the woods and ravines beyond. "After the militia heard the shells and my men had been driven out of the town, it was as much as I could do to hold my position, and impossible to take the offensive," Colonel Runkle later lamented. "I would not move the undrilled militia at all."

Morgan remained concerned by the lack of Union artillery response. Nevertheless, with time running short, he would need to send in his cavalrymen to drive the enemy off Berlin Heights. After an hour-long bombardment, Lawrence's battery ceased fire, and Duke sent three regiments forward in a mounted charge against the Union position. Two regiments moved around Runkle's flanks while the third struck his center. The militia put up a brief resistance. The charge on the Union center was halted at first, but the flanking maneuvers slowly pushed Runkle's disorganized troops into the woods toward the northeast, leaving the Wilkesville–Pomeroy Road wide open. By 2:00 p.m., General Morgan and Duke's brigade disengaged from the fight and rode east to Wilkesville. Before departing town, the raiders burned the Hunsinger & Company flour mill to the ground. The Confederates had suffered four killed and ten wounded. Colonel Runkle never reported any Union casualties. Although Runkle was unable to achieve his original goals, the skirmish at Berlin succeeded in delaying Morgan's march by three hours. At this stage of the raid, every hour was precious to the raiders.

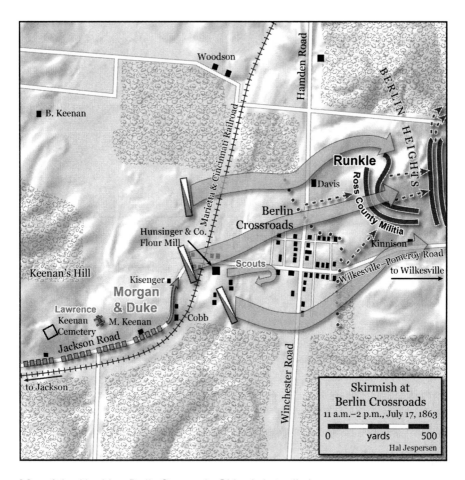

Map of the skirmish at Berlin Crossroads, Ohio. *Author's collection.*

The local home guard offered little resistance other than to annoy the column. Every day since entering the Buckeye State, the militia had sniped at Morgan's men and had chopped down hundreds of trees to block roads. Dealing with these combatants was tiring on the boys, who could do little except disable their enemy's guns and send the Unionists home. Sometimes the raiders forced the locals to clear the felled tree barricades they had built.

Morgan's column reached Wilkesville just before dark. The men ravaged its stores and foraged the area of its horses and food. Morgan stayed at the Dr. William Cline house that night. Dr. Cline's wife was Morgan's first cousin.

Moving out of Wilkesville before dawn on July 18, Morgan sent detachments to Harrisonville and Danville to search for enemy soldiers and to enhance foraging in this mostly remote area of southeast Ohio. Colonel Johnson's brigade rejoined him along the way. Johnson reported the presence of Judah's column, whose Ninth Michigan Cavalry detachment had encountered Johnson's flankers near Centerville. Morgan would need to find a river crossing quickly. The main Confederate column passed through Salem Center, Langsville and Rutland before nearing the river port at Pomeroy. A well-known Ohio River ford at Eight Mile Island near Cheshire and a ferry at Middleport beckoned the men forward. To get to either one, they first needed to brush aside the militia at Middleport.

Defending the roads to Middleport were two companies of the Middleport Militia, 120 men in all, under the command of Captain R.B. Wilson. Supporting them was the Pomeroy Militia under Captain C.W. Smith. They had constructed barricades of felled trees, fence rails and other materials to block the major roads leading to the river. Using these obstacles and the rough wooded terrain to their advantage, the militiamen planned to set a trap for Morgan's Division.

About 9:00 a.m., as the Fourteenth Kentucky Cavalry approached the Middleport Militia's barricade on the Middleport Road, Private Curtis Burke sensed trouble. "The blockade was in a place where the road run between hills, besides it was defended by a strong force of home guards and bushwhackers to prevent our clearing away the obstructions." The raiders waited an hour before deciding it would be too time-consuming to remove the barricade. They backtracked to the Rutland Road and turned east.

Reaching the intersection of the Rutland Road with the Stagecoach Road, Burke's regiment came in contact with another company of the Middleport Militia supported by an artillery piece under the command of Captain John Schreiner. The enemy had placed themselves in ambush along the steep wooded slopes on either side of the narrow Stagecoach Road where it passed over Jacobs Hill, renamed Bradbury Hill after the war. Schreiner's old cannon, formerly used for Fourth of July celebrations and loaded with only scrap metal and nails, covered the road for several hundred yards. East of the intersection, the Pomeroy Militia had barricaded the direct road to Pomeroy. They, too, held a strong position on a "high bluff of rocks" overlooking the intersection. Two companies of the Tenth Kentucky Cavalry came up to assist in driving the Pomeroy Militia back out of shooting range, while other regiments from Johnson's brigade dismounted to feel out the Middleport Militia to the south. Schreiner's cannon let loose its contents, which did little harm other than compel Johnson's veterans to seek shelter.

As the Second Brigade skirmished with the Middleport Militia on Jacobs Hill, General Morgan arrived to assess the situation with Colonel Johnson.

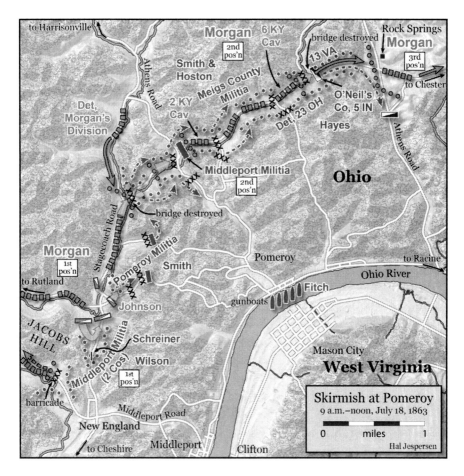

Map of the skirmish at Pomeroy, Ohio. *Author's collection.*

They decided that forcing their way over Jacobs Hill would be too costly in time and men. They abandoned their notion of crossing at Eight Mile Island Ford. Noticing the smoke plumes rising above the hills in the direction of Pomeroy, they rightly concluded there were gunboats docked in town, and possibly enemy soldiers unloading as they spoke. Therefore, they had no other choice but to ride for the ford at Buffington Island, where no enemy gunboats could go this time of year.

To circumvent Pomeroy to get to Buffington Island would prove to be a difficult task. For four miles, the Stagecoach Road led through the narrow Thomas Fork valley bounded on both sides by steep, wooded, rocky hills. For the last two miles, the slopes of these hills abutted the road like the walls of a canyon. Unbeknownst to Morgan, Smith's Pomeroy Militia, including his Trumbull Guards, and Captain H.M. Horton's (Hoston's) Meigs County Militia had perched themselves on these hills, hiding behind rocks and trees at key places where the roads from Pomeroy entered the Stagecoach Road. At every such intersection, the militiamen constructed felled tree barricades to stop the raider column as it moved through the narrow passage. The militia also destroyed bridges for the same purpose. While the Confederate vanguard dealt with clearing obstacles and constructing temporary bridges, Morgan's waiting men would be perfect targets for the snipers in the hills. A veritable gauntlet had been set for Morgan's Division to run.

As Morgan's column moved northeast along the Stagecoach Road, the fighting in the gauntlet became intense, with shots coming from all directions. The Pomeroy and Meigs County militiamen sniped at the Confederate column's front and flanks, while the Middleport Militia from Jacobs Hill nipped at its rear. Here and there, a raider would fall from his saddle. "We were fired on from the hills about all the way through," wrote Private John Weatherred of the Ninth Tennessee. Colonel Basil Duke described how the Confederates handled the situation: "Colonel Grigsby took the lead with the Sixth Kentucky, and dashed through at a gallop, halting when fired on, dismounting his men and dislodging the enemy, and again resuming his rapid march. Major Webber brought up the rear of the division and held back the enemy, who closed eagerly upon our track." At each place where the Confederates drove the enemy away from a barricade, the militia would leapfrog to the next barricade farther up the road. Private Burke wrote, "Every mile or so we would come to places where trees were cut across the road. The advance guard would sing out, 'Sappers and Miners to the front!! Pass it back!!' The sappers and miners would pass us in a jump and go to clearing the road...Sometimes the sappers and miners would be called for in front before finishing their last job. We made all the citizens we could catch help clear the road. In this way the command did not have to wait."

Basil Duke described the skirmish along the Stagecoach Road as "one continual fight." This time, the Confederates faced not only militia, whom the Rebels felt they could lick, but also regulars, whom the raiders knew would give them trouble. In the last mile of the gauntlet, the raiders encountered regular troops in the hills and in their front. Lieutenant John O'Neil's company of fifty picked men from the Fifth Indiana Cavalry suddenly charged Grigsby's Sixth Kentucky. The Kentuckians beat back the smaller Union force, but the fighting was not as easy as with the militia. To make things worse, two battle-hardened infantry regiments had joined in the fray. The Thirteenth Virginia (U.S.) Infantry and the Twenty-third Ohio Infantry, under the command of future general and president of the United States Colonel Rutherford B. Hayes, joined the militia on the wooded hillsides. The bluecoats, whose number included another future U.S. president, Lieutenant William McKinley of the Twenty-third Ohio, fired down on the Confederate column with increased fury. However, in a rare moment of indecision, Colonel Hayes let Morgan's Division escape the trap. It would be Hayes's worst mistake of the war.

About noon, Morgan's long wagon train and its Second Kentucky defenders exited the east end of the gauntlet at Rock Springs. Here a large flat area allowed the cavalrymen to set up a strong skirmish line. Hayes, O'Neil and the militia tested the Confederate line, but they did not attack it with vigor. As Morgan's men dressed their wounds and refreshed themselves at the cool waters of Rock Springs, they counted their losses. The raiders tallied three killed and sixteen wounded. The militia suffered four wounded, while Hayes's brigade listed one wounded soldier from the Twenty-third Ohio. The skirmish at Pomeroy had been a lopsided affair, but Morgan's road to Buffington Island was now open—at least for the time being.

Morgan's Division entered the town of Chester about 1:00 p.m. Here, instead of pressing on to the ford, Morgan decided to take a break. Colonel Johnson saw Morgan sitting on a porch at a store in Chester. He smiled at Johnson and asked him to get off his horse and rest a bit. The general looked cheerfully at Johnson and said, "All our troubles are now over, the river is only twenty-five miles away, and tomorrow we will be on Southern soil." When the Confederate rear guard burned the covered bridge over the Shade River, Morgan's civilian guide used the opportunity to escape. Over ninety minutes were spent looking for another guide that would take them to Buffington Island. Duke and Johnson would later point to the unnecessary stop at Chester as the fatal delay that led to the disaster that soon followed.

Meanwhile, General Hobson's division followed in Morgan's wake and reached Chester after dark on July 18. The Provisional Division was strung out that night along the roads as far back as Rock Springs. Farther south, General Judah's brigade had marched overland from Portsmouth to Pomeroy, reaching the latter place at 4:00 p.m. on July 18. Hearing reports that Morgan had gone in the direction of Buffington Island, Judah decided he would march his men through the night along the river road to Racine, and from there, they would ride for Buffington Island. He hoped to surprise Morgan in the morning.

Cavalry Brigade, 3rd Division, XXIII Corps Brig. Gen. Henry M. Judah
5th Indiana Cavalry [90th Indiana Regiment] Lt. Col. Thomas H. Butler
14th Illinois Cavalry Col. Horace Capron
11th Kentucky (U.S.) Cavalry (1 co.) Major Milton Graham
8th Michigan Cavalry (Co. I) + 9th Michigan Cavalry (Cos. C and K, with detachments from Cos. A and B) Col. James I. David
Battery L, 1st Michigan Light Artillery [11th Michigan Battery] Capt. Charles J. Thompson (two rifled guns)
5th Indiana Cavalry Battery Lt. Charles H. Dumont (two 3-inch ordnance rifles)
14th Illinois Cavalry Battery Lt. DeRiley Kilbourne (four 12-pounder mountain howitzers)
Henshaw's Illinois Independent Battery Light Artillery Capt. Edward C. Henshaw (two 6-pounder brass 3.67-inch howitzers)

After passing through Bashan, the Confederate column fumbled through the dark forested hills made eerie by the oncoming twilight. As the men plodded toward the Portland bottoms and its coveted ford at Buffington Island, they talked among themselves about how good it would be to ride on Southern soil again. They were only a few hours away from freedom—or so they thought.

Chapter 6

"Better Make the Best of It"

The vanguard of Morgan's 1,930-man division emerged onto the Portland bottoms about 8:00 p.m. The scouts headed straight for the Buffington Island Ford to inspect its condition. Before they neared the ford at the head of the island, they spotted a redoubt manned by Union "regular troops" with two formidable-looking brass cannons.

The large earthwork had been constructed over the course of the last two days by a group of green militiamen under the command of Captain D.L. Wood, Eighteenth U.S. Infantry. On July 16, the well-prepared, quick-thinking Union commander at Marietta, Colonel William Putnam, had ordered Captain Wood to assemble two hundred recruits from the city of Marietta and from nearby Athens County, Ohio. A portion of them moved down to Buffington Island on the night of the sixteenth and began digging, while the rest arrived at 6:00 p.m. the next day with two artillery pieces of the Harmar Battery. Wood's Marietta Militia completed the earthwork and its supporting entrenchments well before Morgan's arrival. Wood sent out fifty mounted scouts to scour the region for Morgan's men. They reported Morgan's presence in Chester on the afternoon of the eighteenth.

Earlier that day, Wood had averted disaster when the steamboat *Starlight*, ignoring Fitch's orders to stay off the river, lodged onto a sand bar near Buffington Island. Knowing well how Morgan had employed captured steamboats at Brandenburg, Wood quickly put his men to work removing cargo from the vessel to lighten its load. When the *Starlight* was freed from the bar, Wood commandeered the boat for his own use.

After Morgan's scouts reported that an entrenched enemy blocked the way to the coveted ford, General Morgan had to make a tough decision. The scouts had seen what appeared to be several hundred troops with a battery, but with darkness setting in, it was hard to tell how many of them there were. Wood had done his best to deceive Morgan by spreading his two hundred militiamen over the full length of the earthworks and placing pickets in front of them. Couriers also had informed Morgan that the Ohio River depth was very high—a twenty-year high, according to one elderly local woman. Heavy rains in the hills of western Pennsylvania had flooded the headwaters of the Ohio, and all that water had surged downriver to Buffington Island. What had been a river depth of only thirty inches a week earlier was now a raging five to six feet! Fording the flooded river at night would be dangerous, even for experienced riders. Duke suggested that they drive off the Union force with a night attack, abandon the wagon train and the wounded and swim the rest of the men across throughout the night. However, Morgan would have none of that. It was all or nothing for him. He would not abandon his wounded men to the enemy, and a night attack was too risky. Besides, the men were dangerously low on ammunition, averaging five rounds per man. Morgan decided they would encamp for the night on the Portland bottoms, and at first light, they would capture the redoubt and ford the river.

Colonel Duke was given the task of capturing the Union redoubt in the morning. He placed the Fifth and Sixth Kentucky into a semicircular line about four hundred yards from the redoubt and directed Lieutenant Elias Lawrence to unlimber his two Parrott rifles on a small grassy knoll eight hundred yards west of the earthwork. Duke's Kentuckians lay on their arms all night while the rest of the men in the division fell to the cold, damp earth in the corn and wheat fields on either side of the Chester Road. The soldiers were told to extinguish their fires so as not to reveal their position to the gunboats downriver. Men from the Ninth Tennessee and Fourteenth Kentucky went to work scrounging up any available rafts or boats they could find and preparing them for use, much like they had done prior to crossing the Cumberland so many weeks before. A dense fog moved in. It would be a restless night for many of these brave Confederate soldiers. Despite their fatigue, they had a difficult time sleeping. They knew they were only yards away from freedom, yet so many of their enemies were closing in from all directions. Would they beat their Union pursuers to West Virginia? "All night long every one of us that I heard express themselves said we would be captured, many of us, if we remained all night," remembered Private Weatherred. Even with Morgan at the helm, they felt a sense of impending doom.

None of the raiders understood just how close their pursuers were or how many of them were about to pounce. During the dark, foggy night of July 18, as Morgan's men slept on the banks of the Ohio, all the land-based and water-based Union forces were on the move. However, none of the Union commanders knew where the others were at that moment; they only knew Morgan was at Buffington Island. At about 8:00 p.m., General Hobson's vanguard, commanded by Colonel August Kautz, reached Chester, where they rested for a few hours before setting off for Portland. Farther to the south, General Judah's column rode into Pomeroy. General Eliakim P. Scammon briefed Judah on the day's action and advised him of Morgan's apparent move toward Buffington Island. Judah decided to make a night march to the island using the Pomeroy–Portland Road, which passed through Racine before approaching the foot of the island from the south. Meanwhile, Lieutenant Commander Fitch had the lightweight dispatch boat *Imperial* tow his heavily armed flag boat USS *Moose* from the mouth of Sandy Creek over a sand bar toward the chute, or waterway, separating Buffington Island from the Ohio shoreline. Not long after 2:00 a.m., the *Moose* and the *Imperial* anchored below the foot of the island, the dense fog preventing them from going any farther.

The Rebels knew that Fitch's boats had anchored three miles downstream at the Sandy Creek Shoals near Ravenswood, but since Duke had somehow failed to post pickets on the Pomeroy–Portland Road, the Confederates were unaware of the new position of Fitch's gunboat. Yet some of the raiders clearly heard the steam emanating from its boilers. Soon afterward, the makeshift gunboat *Allegheny Belle* appeared off *Moose*'s stern. The *Belle* was armed with Captain Charles J. Thompson's two artillery pieces from the Eleventh Michigan Battery, along with a ten-pounder Parrott rifle mounted on the boat's bow. Fitch ordered the *Belle*'s pilot, John Sebastian, to moor the steamboat nearby and prepare for action.

Shrouded by the heavy fog in the pre-dawn hours of Sunday, July 19, Captain Wood quietly led his men out of the redoubt and along the riverbank a third of a mile to where the steamer *Starlight* awaited them. Before abandoning the earthworks, his men spiked the Harmar Battery guns and manually dumped them over the steep riverbank. Mysteriously, the sounds of the rolling cannons and the bursting steam of the *Starlight* missed detection by Morgan's men. Wood's heroes would land safely in Ravenswood, West Virginia, before sunrise.

At dawn on July 19, Colonel Duke led the Fifth and Sixth Kentucky dismounted toward the Union redoubt. All were surprised to find the earthworks empty and the cannons lying broken amid the tangled brush at the bottom of the riverbank. Duke sent word back to Morgan that the way was clear and that the crossing procedures could begin. Meanwhile, believing the Union soldiers had withdrawn down the Pomeroy Road, Duke ordered Colonel Dabney Howard Smith to lead the Fifth and Sixth Kentucky Cavalries southward in dismounted battle formation to discover where the elusive militiamen had gone.

About 110 men of the Ninth Tennessee Cavalry, under Captain John D. Kirkpatrick, floated across the Ohio River on a flatboat and four skiffs. They left their horses on the Ohio side with the intention that they would ferry them later. The two companies deployed on the high wooded ridge overlooking the West Virginia end of the ford. Their mission was to set up a defensive perimeter to cover the crossing for the rest of the division.

While Kirkpatrick ferried his men across the river, General Judah "slowly and cautiously" led his mounted bodyguard, Company G, Fifth Indiana Cavalry, and a single gun of Henshaw's Illinois Battery northward along the Pomeroy–Portland Road. Accompanying them at the front of the column was Major Daniel McCook, patriarch of the famous "Fighting McCooks" of Ohio. He had joined General Judah's staff in Cincinnati as a volunteer aide-de-camp and paymaster. As a former law partner of President Lincoln's secretary of war, Edwin Stanton, McCook's notoriety had helped convince General Burnside to give him a position on Judah's staff for the purpose of tracking down Morgan's raiders. Old Dan McCook sought revenge against the raiders. He believed one of them had killed his son, Brigadier General Robert L. McCook, in cold blood in 1862 while he was lying in an ambulance in northern Alabama. To face Morgan's men was an opportunity Dan had only dreamed about.

About 5:30 a.m., Smith's Kentuckians accidently collided with the vanguard of General Judah's brigade. The dense fog prevented anyone from seeing beyond fifty yards. As a result, the opposing forces were equally surprised to discover each other. Unfortunately for Judah's severely exposed contingent, Smith's dismounted troopers had the upper hand in the initial contact. The raiders instantly fired a volley at point-blank range into the head of Judah's force, killing two privates; wounding ten men and Judah's aide-de-camp, Lieutenant Fred G. Price; and mortally wounding Major Dan McCook, who fell off his horse into the road. The Confederate line wrapped around the Union column, which could not deploy into line because of the tall sturdy

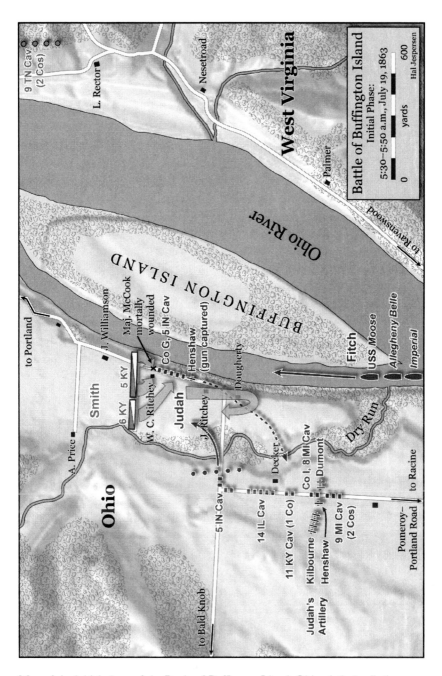

Map of the initial phase of the Battle of Buffington Island, Ohio. *Author's collection.*

fences bordering the roadway. The cannon from Henshaw's Battery overturned in the road, blocking the escape route for Judah and his Hoosier cavalrymen. Judah managed to get away on the back of a horse, but Captain Edward Henshaw, his cannon and thirty other officers and men were captured.

Colonel Smith's men charged after the retreating Federals on the road and through the adjoining fields of the Ritchey farms. As the raiders flooded through the yard of the Dougherty house, they were met with a disheartening sight. The breathless General Judah directed his cavalrymen to deploy for battle, and as the fog lifted, Smith could see the long line of blue-clad cavalrymen on the Pomeroy Road beyond the far edge of Dougherty's field. A spattering of shots from Judah's pickets were enough to convince Smith to retreat back to his position near the head of Buffington Island, where he would receive support and further orders from Duke.

Meanwhile, Fitch heard the heavy musketry up the chute off his port bow. Just before 6:00 a.m., he ordered the USS *Moose* to steam slowly up the chute while the *Allegheny Belle* followed close behind. The *Imperial* tagged along at the back of the convoy to assist in any towing that might be needed. Together, they pushed northward up the chute. Soon they were hailed by Judah's aide-de-camp, Captain John Grafton, who had escaped capture during the mêlée at the Ritchey farm. The officer came aboard the *Moose* and offered to aim the fire of its guns in the direction that he knew Smith's men had gone.

Colonel Duke, flabbergasted by the news of Judah's cavalry, ordered Smith to form the Fifth and Sixth Kentucky into line of battle at his original position four hundred yards south of the redoubt. Smith did so, arranging a thin line from the Adams house on the east to the river hills on the west. Together, the two regiments barely totaled five hundred men. Behind the Sixth Kentucky's right flank, Lawrence's battery unleashed its shells on the Union cavalrymen in the distance. Colonel Duke galloped north to consult with General Morgan at his headquarters in the Tunis Middleswart house.

A half mile to the south of Smith's position, General Judah dismounted his cavalrymen into line at the Williamson farm. They were supported by three batteries of artillery stretched across the narrow Portland valley. Judah's force contained about one thousand men. As the Rebel cannons threw shells into their position, the Union artillery responded in kind. The highly accurate fire of Lieutenant Charles H. Dumont's two three-inch ordnance rifles and Lieutenant DeRiley Kilbourne's four twelve-pounder mountain howitzers wrought havoc on Lawrence's gunners, who soon sought cover to escape the heavy bombardment. Private Alfred Austin of the Fifth Indiana Cavalry wrote, "Our battery was brought to play upon them and from the first shot skedaddled like a scarred [sic] flock of sheap [sic]. Our battery playing on them all the time killing from 5 to 8 everey [sic] shot."

About 6:00 a.m., Judah's troopers, armed with carbines and pistols, advanced steadily over the Anderson Price and Adams farms despite the heavy fire from the Fifth and Sixth Kentucky regiments. These Federal soldiers were anxious to make up for the action they had missed for most of the raid. Smith's Kentuckians gradually fell back under the weight of the Union attack. Without orders, Lieutenant John O'Neil's company of crack Fifth Indiana cavalrymen, fresh from their encounter with Morgan at Pomeroy, suddenly mounted a saber charge on Lawrence's battery. Henshaw's artillery piece, taken earlier that morning, sat nearby. With portions of Colonel Horace Capron's Fourteenth Illinois Cavalry and Lieutenant Colonel Thomas H. Butler's Fifth Indiana Cavalry in support, O'Neil's unit successfully captured the guns and scattered the Confederate artillerymen. Minutes later, Colonel Grigsby led a mounted charge of his own to try to recapture the guns. As several companies of horsemen from the Sixth Kentucky Cavalry bounded up the knoll with their revolvers blazing, the Illinois and Indiana cavalrymen fired a well-aimed volley from their kneeling position. Horses reeled, and men toppled from their saddles. Grigsby and his survivors withdrew. The Parrott rifles fell into the hands of their enemy.

At this time, Colonel Duke returned from headquarters only to find Smith's situation had deteriorated. Without the artillery to support him, he had no choice but to retreat to a new position. As he reformed the Fifth and Sixth Kentucky in the fields west of the ford, Duke called for the Second Kentucky Cavalry to support his weakened line in the valley. The regiment never came. However, the Fourteenth Kentucky Cavalry and Captain Byrne's two howitzers moved forward along the Portland Road to fill the gap between the Fifth Kentucky and the river.

About 6:15 a.m., the USS *Moose* fired its two twenty-four-pounder Dahlgren cannons located in the bow of the gunboat. Duke and his men were startled by the unexpected appearance of the gunboat and the loud report of its Dahlgrens. Fitch had spotted Byrne's guns racing south toward the head of Buffington Island. Fitch assumed that they would be used to stop the gunboat's advance up the chute. The shells from the Dahlgrens burst near the Confederate howitzers before they had time to unlimber. Realizing that he was outgunned by the *Moose*, which hosted six twenty-four-pounder Dahlgren boat howitzers, Byrne wheeled his battery section around and rode off toward Portland. After the *Moose* cleared the north end of the chute, the *Allegheny Belle* had room to add its fire to the mix. Its three cannons inflicted equal damage

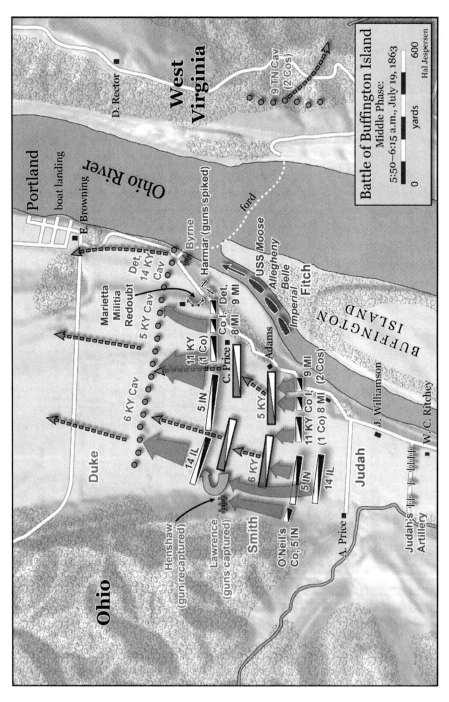

Map of the middle phase of the Battle of Buffington Island, Ohio. *Author's collection.*

A rare photograph of the gunboat USS *Moose*, which served as Lieutenant Commander Le Roy Fitch's flag boat. The *Moose* played a significant role in the defeat of Morgan's Division at Buffington Island. Note the twenty-four-pounder Dahlgren boat howitzer on the top deck. *Courtesy of Larry M. Strayer Collection.*

to Duke's wavering line. Under pressure from Judah's cavalrymen and artillery to his front, and now from the Union gunboats on his left, Duke retreated to a new location nearer to Colonel Johnson's position along the Chester Road.

Johnson's and Duke's lines formed at right angles to each other, creating an L-shaped defensive position. The interior of the "L" was crammed with Morgan's other regiments, which were too disorganized to get into action. This area turned into a scene of pandemonium as men on foot and horseback darted from side to side, and back and forth, to escape the bursting Union cannonballs. "There were many stragglers," Duke said, "who were circling about the valley in a delirium of fright, clinging instinctively, in all their terror, to bolts of calico and holding on to led horses, but changing the direction in which they galloped, with every shell which whizzed or burst near them." Somehow, General Morgan was able to extricate most of his men from this deadly arena with some semblance of order.

Hidden among the bushes on the West Virginia hills, Captain Kirkpatrick and his Tennesseans watched in horror as the battle unfolded across the river. "We saw it all," recalled Private Weatherred. "The only battle I witnessed during the war, because I was usually in it and not in a position to see much...We saw my regiment, Ward's 9th Tennessee and the 2nd Ky. Dukes Reg. captured and many others." General Scammon sent Hayes's brigade by steamboat up to Buffington Island to search for Morgan's refugees. When one of these Union regiments passed within yards of the Tennesseans, they silently abandoned their perch on the river. They would walk nearly two hundred miles through the West Virginia mountains to reach Confederate lines at Dublin Depot, Virginia.

Between 6:00 and 6:15 a.m., Union colonel Kautz's brigade engaged Johnson's men on the Chester Road above the Portland bottoms. An hour earlier, Kautz's advance pickets had encountered Colonel Johnson's pickets two miles west of Morgan's camp. Alerted to this fact, an excited Colonel Kautz immediately mounted the two hundred best men of his brigade and led them to the sound of the guns. In the meantime, Johnson scrambled the Seventh Kentucky Cavalry into a skirmish line along the ridge above their camp. Soon, the reduced-size Union brigade, consisting of detachments from the Second and Seventh Ohio Cavalry regiments, ran headlong into the Rebel skirmishers. Kautz dismounted his Buckeyes into a skirmish line and easily drove the disorganized Confederates back onto Johnson's main line forming in the valley below. Colonel Johnson arranged the bulk of the Seventh Kentucky and Tenth Kentucky across the Chester Road to check Kautz's advance. The raiders held their position until the arrival of Colonel Sanders and his Michigan brigade at about 6:30 a.m.

While Kautz occupied the Confederates' attention on the Chester Road, General Hobson hurried forward Sanders's brigade containing portions of the Eighth and Ninth Michigan Cavalry regiments and a section of rifled artillery from the Eleventh Michigan Battery. The general rode onto the field with Sanders's Michiganders as it formed into a skirmish line behind Kautz's Ohioans. Sanders ordered Lieutenant Roys's Eleventh Michigan Battery to unlimber its two rifled guns ahead of the cavalrymen. One gun opened fire from a rise on the Chester Road within six hundred yards of Johnson's men. The other piece found an excellent position on a cleared knoll at the west end of Tunis Middleswart's farm lane. The gunners "witnessed a grand panorama"—a wide-open plain packed tightly with the disorganized regiments of Morgan's Division. It was an artilleryman's dream come true. Now Morgan's Division was hit by artillery fire from three sides. Roys's guns delivered deadly accurate shells and shrapnel into Morgan's mass of troopers and wagons, but the Union artillery's best contribution that day was the enfilade fire on Duke's brigade.

Lieutenant Commander Fitch's two gunboats, USS *Moose* and *Allegheny Belle*, with the *Imperial* trailing in reserve, steamed upriver and centered

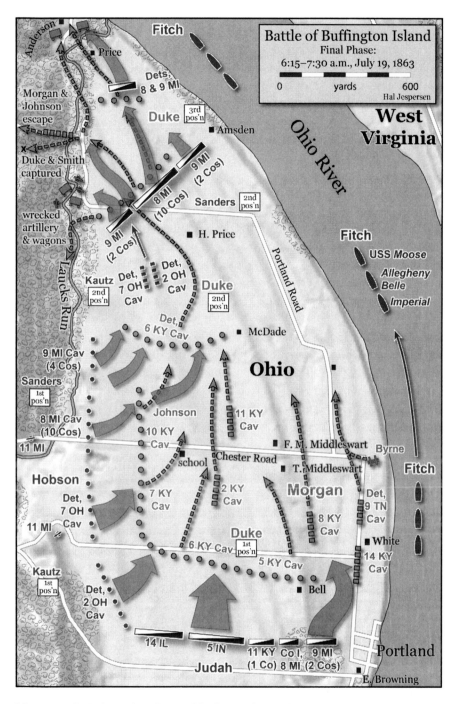

Map of the final phase of the Battle of Buffington Island, Ohio. *Author's collection.*

themselves along Duke's left flank, at which point they fired broadsides into the Kentuckians. The gunboats also lobbed shells into the mass of Confederate troopers forming in column behind General Morgan, who led them across the Middleswart, McDade and Price farm fields to the Portland Road exit at the northern end of the valley. Although most of Fitch's shots hit the enemy, some projectiles landed among Union troopers, causing confusion in their ranks. The thick smoke and high riverbanks often obscured the battle lines from the navy spotters. In many cases, the cannoneers guessed the aim of their Dahlgren howitzers.

When Byrne's relocated artillery fired errant shots at the naval vessels, the gunboats responded with an accurate barrage that forced the Confederate artillery to withdraw again. Frustrated by the gunboats, Colonel Duke "heartily wished that *their* fierce ardor, the result of a feeling of perfect security, could have been subjected to the test of two or three shots through their hulls." Fitch's deadly broadsides caused the Fourteenth Kentucky to remount and break for the rear, opening a gap of three hundred yards between the river and the Fifth Kentucky's left flank. Smith's Fifth Kentucky could not withstand the extreme pressure of the enfilade fire from Fitch's gunboats on one flank and the Eleventh Michigan Battery on the other. With the added strain of Judah's Michigan cavalrymen turning his left flank, Smith withdrew his Kentuckians northward, leaving the Sixth Kentucky exposed. Judah's and Kautz's forces nearly surrounded the regiment before it cut its way out and retired northward. Major William Bullitt and his group of stalwart Sixth Kentuckians executed at least three rear guard actions against Sanders's and Kautz's brigades to buy time for the rest of Morgan's Division to escape up the Portland Road.

As Bullitt's Sixth Kentucky detachment delayed the overwhelming numbers of converging Union troopers, Duke and Johnson conferred about their next move. With General Morgan having successfully left the battlefield with over half of the division, Duke and Johnson were the highest-ranking officers on the field. Duke decided to conduct a last stand at the point where the Portland Road entered the deep ravine formed by Lauck's Run, a shallow creek that flowed north into the Ohio River. Johnson would lead the rest of the men off the field to safety.

As artillery shot and shell continued to rain down on the Confederates from the Union field batteries as well as Fitch's gunboats, some of Morgan's wagons in the rear were overturned by the projectiles. One cannonball bowled over a wagon on the Portland Road, blocking the Confederates' main escape route. The men in the rear panicked and broke for Lauck's Run ravine. The largest group raced for the place where the Portland Road made its sharp turn down into the ravine. Here, wagons, ambulances, caissons and Byrne's artillery pieces careened off the road and rolled down the twenty-five-foot cliff into the creek below, where they settled into a large pile of wreckage. Mingled with the smashed vehicles and their spilled contents were the mutilated corpses of horses and men who had gone down with them. The other group turned north through the fields of the Price homestead. When detachments of the Eighth and Ninth Michigan chased after the raiders, some Rebels turned to fight while the rest rode pell-mell into the ravine at the mouth of Lauck's Run. They slid their horses down the steep slope; some of the riders struck trees and were knocked off their steeds. Carriages, buggies and wagons crashed to the bottom of the ravine. Fitch's gunboats followed them upriver and fired grapeshot into the troopers retreating north along the beach. About twenty or thirty Rebels successfully forded the river above the White farm and near the mouth of Lauck's Run, including Captain Byrne, but the gunboats' shells and small arms fire forced most back to the Ohio shore. Many Confederates abandoned their horses and vehicles and ran into the woods, where they were picked up by Union ground forces. Fitch later reported he had captured two artillery pieces abandoned on the beach near the Anderson house, but the army's records do not support this claim.

Colonels Duke and Johnson courageously formed about one to two hundred men from four different regiments into a dismounted line that ran diagonally across the Portland Road. With the chaos occurring in their rear, they realized they had little hope of escaping. Through their determined efforts, they held back the bulk of the Eighth Michigan and Ninth Michigan for fifteen to twenty minutes before running out of ammunition. The Michiganders overpowered and outflanked Duke's line on both ends. Johnson escaped with a portion of the rear guard, but Duke remained behind with the rest. The Michigan cavalrymen's Spencer rifles proved destructive in this final phase of the fight. Many raiders gave their lives on this part of the battlefield.

By 7:00 a.m., Duke's line had dissolved into Lauck's Run ravine. Colonel Duke and Colonel D.H. Smith huddled quietly in an adjoining ravine with fifty of their men and officers, hoping to remain undetected by the pursuing Federals until nightfall, when they could make their escape. Their hopes were dashed a half hour later when a Union cavalryman spotted their tracks at the top of the ravine. Duke, Smith and their remaining raiders surrendered to a Michigan officer. The Battle of Buffington Island was over.

Morgan's Division suffered 57 killed, 63 wounded and 50 captured on the field. General Hobson cared for the Confederates' wounded and buried their dead in a mass grave on the battlefield. Duke's last stand at Lauck's Run had allowed

1,050 cavalrymen to escape with General Morgan and Colonel Johnson. The remaining 570 men of Morgan's Division were scattered across eastern Meigs County. About 470 of them, including Lieutenant Colonel John Huffman and most of the other 100 wounded men who rode away from the battlefield, would be captured over the course of the next twenty-four hours by various Union militia and regular troops. The prisoners were collected at Portland, Pomeroy and Cheshire and were transported by steamboat to Cincinnati. From there, the Rebels were sent to prisoner-of-war camps across the North.

Union casualties were comparatively light. The Federals totaled fifty-five killed and wounded. All of the men and officers captured in the initial phase of the battle had been liberated near the Tunis Middleswart house, where Morgan's adjutant was in the act of paroling them before the battle swept him away.

A newspaper correspondent described the Portland bottoms after the action had ended:

> *The battlefield and roads surrounding it were strewn with a thousand articles never seen on a battlefield before. One is accustomed to seeing broken swords, muskets and bayonets, haversacks, cartridge boxes, belts, pistols, gun carriages, cannons, wagons upset, wounded, dead and dying on the battlefield, but besides all these on the battlefield at Buffington Island, one could pick up almost any article in dry goods, hardware, house furnishing or ladies or gentlemen's furnishing line. Hats, boots, gloves, knives, forks, spoons, calico, ribbons, drinking cups, buggies, carriages, a circus wagon, and an almost endless variety of articles, useful and all, more or less, valuable.*

General Judah met with General Hobson at Portland while cleanup duties were underway. Judah attempted to reclaim his command superiority over Hobson, but Hobson referred back to Burnside's July 6 special orders, which were still in effect until Burnside changed them. Frustrated, Judah telegraphed Burnside at 1:00 p.m. and argued for his command status to be restored: "My position as his [Hobson's] division commander, with an inferior force to his, and both distinct and separate and operating together is anomalous, and, under the circumstances, I cannot believe that you desire to maintain me in it." Burnside replied sternly but politely:

> *Don't allow anything to stop the pursuit and capture of the enemy. Either Hobson or yourself have sufficient force to do this, and either one that retards this will assume a heavy responsibility, which will bring its retribution. Again I say the enemy must be pursued and captured. General Hobson has*

Union brigadier general James M. Shackelford led the final stage of the pursuit of Morgan's raiders. Justifiably, he claimed to be Morgan's captor, but subordinate Major George Rue took the credit. Shackelford resigned from the army in 1864. He replaced "Hanging Judge" Isaac Parker in 1889. *Courtesy of U.S. Army HEC, MOLLUS Collection.*

been in pursuit for many days, and he has done a good work, and he must not be balked. You understand my wishes, and I am sure you will carry them out. I thank you both for the work already done.

Fuming over Burnside's support of Hobson, Judah went to Pomeroy to attend to other affairs. He refused to participate in the pursuit of Morgan from this point forward. Unfortunately, because of Judah's interference and delay, Hobson would be unable to assist personally in catching Morgan. This job would be left in the hands of Hobson's brigade commanders, the most senior of them being Brigadier General James Shackelford.

James Murrell Shackelford celebrated his thirty-sixth birthday on July 7 while not far away from his birthplace at Danville, Kentucky. Colleagues described him as "brave to the verge of rashness, always capable of making the best disposition of his forces, a good disciplinarian, yet much beloved by his men for his magnanimous impulses." A Mexican-American War veteran and a well-respected lawyer, Shackelford raised the Twenty-fifth Kentucky (U.S.) Infantry at the beginning of the Civil War. As its colonel, he led it gallantly at the Siege of Fort Donelson, but because of health problems, he resigned his commission. After recovering, he raised the Eighth Kentucky (U.S.) Cavalry. In a battle with Confederate colonel Adam R. Johnson's cavalry at Geiger's Lake, Kentucky, Shackelford's left foot "was torn to pieces by a slug fired from a cannon." After five weeks in the hospital, he returned to his command to fight again. And that he did. His successful encounters with Confederate partisans under such leaders as Johnson and Forrest made Shackelford a rising star in the West, and Lincoln promoted him to a brigadier general of cavalry on January 1, 1863.

Hobson's and Judah's cavalrymen hunted down the Rebels who had escaped Buffington Island. Hobson ordered Shackelford to reverse his brigade and net any raiders retreating west from Portland. Judah's regiments covered the southern avenues of escape. With the Confederates scattered like broken glass across eastern Meigs County, the regulars had difficulty tracking them down on their own. In this situation, the Union militia was very effective in rounding up the renegades.

Among the Confederates roaming the countryside was a large contingent led by General Morgan's brother, Colonel Richard C. Morgan. Colonel Morgan and about 180 men from different regiments took a wrong turn at Long Run. Instead of heading north to Long Bottom with General Morgan's column, they rode west toward Bashan Church. About 9:00 a.m., they encountered the rear guard of General James M. Shackelford's brigade positioned at the crossroads village of Bashan. Colonel Morgan's videttes fired on the Union cavalrymen, who returned the fire and established a skirmish line. A courier was sent to General Shackelford near Chester to inform him that contact had been made with the enemy. In the meantime, Shackelford's cavalry regiments joined in the skirmish one by one.

General Shackelford soon arrived on the scene, accompanied by Colonel Wolford with his First Kentucky (U.S.) Cavalry and Forty-fifth Ohio (Mounted) Infantry regiments. Shackelford arranged the men into a line along the Bashan–Adams Mill Road, from which several of the units had been fighting for some time. Colonel Morgan had placed his men in dense woods and in an old field several hundred yards east of the village. The skirmishing continued for about an hour, at which time Shackelford ordered the three center cavalry regiments—the First Kentucky (U.S.), the Eighth Kentucky (U.S.) and the battalion of the Third Kentucky (U.S.)—to mount their horses and draw their sabers. Lieutenant Colonel Holloway would lead them in the assault. Holloway sounded the charge, and in one gallant rush, the blue-clad horsemen galloped down the hill in perfect order. "With drawn sabers gleaming in the bright sunlight, and a yell that filled the foe with terror, they rushed upon him, and he fled at their approach," observed Shackelford. A reporter noted that the Confederates "broke and scattered like sheep, without firing a shot."

Colonel Morgan was slightly wounded in the fight. Most of his men were out of ammunition and could not return fire on the awesome blue cavalry line. They could only make a beeline for the dense woods where the bluecoats

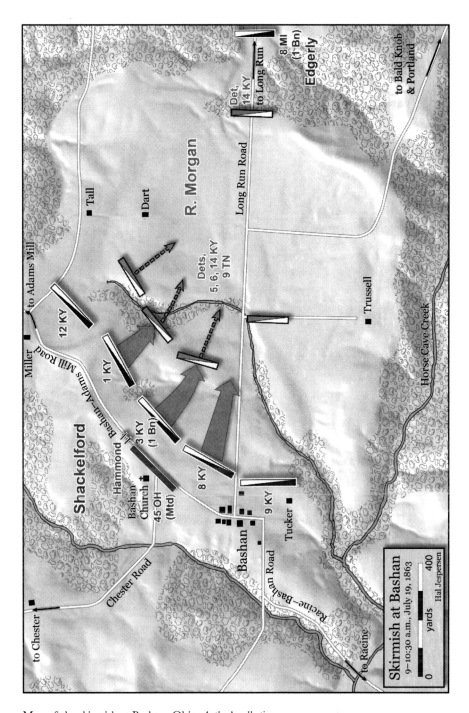

Map of the skirmish at Bashan, Ohio. *Author's collection.*

Confederate colonel Richard C. Morgan, commander of the Fourteenth Kentucky Cavalry, also known as Morgan's Scouts. Richard was one of five Morgan brothers who participated in the Great Raid. Richard was captured on the raid in Ohio and at Kingsport, Tennessee, in 1864. *Courtesy of Hunt-Morgan House Deposit, University of Kentucky.*

could not easily get to them. That did not stop the soldiers of the First Kentucky (U.S.) Cavalry, who constantly pulled prisoners out of the woods. At about the same time, a Union force appeared in Colonel Morgan's rear. A detachment of the Fourteenth Kentucky served as the rear guard on the Long Run Road. Major Henry C. Edgerly and his battalion of the Eighth Michigan Cavalry attacked them, but the Kentuckians held their ground.

About 10:30 a.m., Colonel Morgan realized there was nothing more he could do. His men were completely surrounded, and they had no ammunition to cut their way out. He sent a flag of truce to General Shackelford, who demanded an unconditional surrender of Morgan's group. Colonel Morgan accepted. He ordered his men to mount and ride single file into the Union lines—and into captivity—at Bashan. Private Curtis Burke of the Fourteenth Kentucky remembered his capture at Bashan:

While Col. Dick Morgan was making the conditions of our surrender, we threw away nearly everything that we had got on the raid. All of the pistols were thrown as far into the bushes as we could throw them. Some were thrown away in pieces. I met Pa looking as if he had lost something. I laughed and told him that we were trapped and had better make the best of it. Some of the boys even threw away greenbacks and watches for fear that the Yanks would treat them rough if they found such things about them. We cleared our saddles of everything new. There was enough things scattered through the woods to set up quite a respectable variety store.

With tear-filled eyes, Colonel Richard Morgan surrendered with several other officers, including Colonel William W. Ward of the Ninth Tennessee Cavalry, Major William P. Elliott of General Morgan's staff and Lieutenant Leeland Hathaway of the scouts.

Following the disaster at Buffington Island, General Morgan and the 1,050-man remnant of his division attained relative safety at Long Bottom, an Ohio River village located seven miles upstream from Portland. Here he rested his demoralized and weary men while he waited for the scattered remnants of his division to trickle in. Only a few would come. Morgan was downtrodden by the loss of so many good officers and men, including his most trusted companion, Basil Duke. Nevertheless, his primary objective had not changed. Morgan needed to get his men over the Ohio River.

Morgan's first order of business was to reorganize his remaining troopers. While Colonel Johnson retained his leadership of the Second Brigade, Morgan assigned command of the First Brigade to the tough, fearless Major Thomas Webber.

Twenty-nine-year-old Thomas Binford Webber hailed from Byhalia, Mississippi, where he owned a successful mercantile business. Throughout his life, Thomas suffered from chronic bouts of sickness, but he did not let it stop him from accomplishing his goals. He became highly educated and enjoyed traveling and constant activity. At the start of the Civil War, he joined the Ninth Mississippi Infantry, but after his brother was killed at the Battle of Santa Rosa Island, Florida, in 1861, he deserted. In the spring of 1862, he formed a company of mounted soldiers designated as Company F, Second Kentucky Cavalry, within John Hunt Morgan's command. Since many of the company's members were transfers from his old outfit in the Ninth Mississippi, Webber's unit was nicknamed the "Mississippi Company." Morgan and Duke often cited Webber and Company F for their bravery in battle and their discipline on the march. In fact, Duke referred to Webber as the "fiery major." "I have acquired a morbid fondness for action," Webber admitted. "Nothing short of being continually stressed up to the full extent of my mental and physical capabilities will satisfy me at all." At the start of the Great Raid, the command of the Second Kentucky Cavalry devolved on Webber when Lieutenant Colonel James Bowles became physically unable to stay with the regiment.

With Fitch's gunboats close on his heels, Morgan led his reorganized division upstream to the Belleville Island Ford at Reedsville, reaching there on the afternoon of July 19. He ordered Colonel Adam Johnson to begin crossing the men through the swirling, debris-choked waters of the flooded Ohio. The raging stream nearly swept Johnson away, but he managed to swim his horse to the West Virginia shore. Not all of the raiders following him were as lucky. Several men drowned in the attempt, their floating hats marking their watery graves.

Confederate major Thomas B. Webber led the Second Kentucky Cavalry and received command of the First Brigade after Buffington Island. His men called him "Iron Man" because he refused to let his severe chronic illness keep him out of the saddle. *Courtesy of Cowan's Auctions Inc., Cincinnati, Ohio.*

Suddenly, Lieutenant Commander Fitch's gunboats appeared around the bend. Because the river depth was dropping, the *Imperial* towed the USS *Moose* upriver from Portland, with the *Allegheny Belle* trailing close behind. Fitch saw the Confederates fording the stream. Morgan was swimming his horse in midstream when the *Moose* came into sight. Looking over his shoulder at the hundreds of raiders trapped on the Ohio shore, he decided to turn back and rejoin them. He would share their fate. No man would be left behind, he thought.

When Fitch saw the Rebels disappear into the Ohio interior, he ordered his sailors to hold their fire on the raiders still thrashing in the water or huddling along the West Virginia shore. This humane act saved several Confederates' lives. Colonel Johnson, Colonel Grigsby, George "Lightning" Ellsworth and a little over three hundred men managed to reach the West Virginia shore. They escaped into the mountains and successfully navigated their way to friendly territory in Virginia later that month. With Johnson gone, Morgan placed Colonel Roy S. Cluke in charge of the Second Brigade.

Morgan was determined to cross the river. Another mile upstream, his vanguard began wading through the river at Lee Creek Ford, but only a handful of men reached the other side before Fitch's gunboats came up and fired a round or two into them, killing and wounding several of the Confederates. Morgan rode northward two miles farther and tried again, but Fitch prevented the Confederates from getting far into the water. Being only a few miles from the heavily defended town of Hockingport, and with darkness approaching, Morgan would not risk another attempt. He turned his column of roughly eight hundred men inland in the hopes of crossing the river somewhere else.

Chapter 7

Five Hundred Volunteers

While Morgan searched for a way to get over the Ohio River, General Hobson ordered Shackelford to lead the pursuit of Morgan. Shackelford carried with him six hundred troopers of Wolford's brigade and his own, along with Law's four-gun Mountain Howitzer Battery. Ohio militia units joined them along the way.

Not long after Morgan turned inland from the river, Shackelford's troops entered the hamlet of Tuppers Plains. At once, Shackelford blocked the Confederate leader's path by placing his men across the main road leading west from Reedsville. North of Morgan's position, large groups of militia and a detachment of the Seventh Ohio Cavalry guarded all of the Hocking River fords from Hockingport to Coolville. East of Morgan's men, the Twenty-third Ohio Infantry scoured the hills along the west bank of the river. In the meantime, Hobson's and Judah's cavalry closed in on Morgan from the south. Morgan's raiders were surrounded. The Rebel general told his men to make camp while he devised a plan to solve their predicament.

Shackelford and Wolford conducted a personal reconnaissance of Morgan's position at Flatwoods, a small crossroads community three miles southeast of Tuppers Plains. Flatwoods sat on top of a high, densely wooded ridge that was well suited for defense against cavalry attacks. Any assault that Shackelford could make would be done dismounted and without artillery. As darkness approached, the Union general decided it was best to wait until dawn to fight.

Morgan waited until dark to make his next move. Throughout the night, he ordered his raiders to light campfires in the fields surrounding

Flatwoods. About 11:00 p.m., with their fires burning brightly, he arranged his cavalrymen into single file. Mounted on his horse, Glencoe, Morgan led them silently down a steep ravine along a small, nondescript wagon trail that Shackelford's pickets had failed to guard. As the raiders crept along, they could see the enemy's campfires within shouting distance of them.

Morgan's remnants rode around Shackelford's northern flank during the night. By dawn, they had reached a point four miles west of Tuppers Plains before Union pickets reported that the raiders had vanished. Earlier that morning, Lieutenant Colonel James Comly and his Twenty-third Ohio charged into Morgan's former camp and discovered fifty sick and wounded Confederates who had volunteered to stay behind to stoke the campfires all night. Shackelford had been duped.

Shackelford ordered an immediate pursuit. Morgan passed through Harrisonville, where he briefly rested his men and replenished their horses and supplies. He turned south and rode swiftly through Rutland toward Kygerville. Along the way, over one hundred stragglers from Buffington Island joined his column. Morgan's plan was to ford his troopers across the Ohio River at Cheshire's Eight Mile Island.

Shackelford's column, led by the redoubtable Frank Wolford, caught up to Morgan's rear guard outside Kygerville. For the next six miles, Wolford's forward regiment, the Forty-fifth Ohio (Mounted) Infantry, skirmished continuously with Lieutenant Colonel Cicero Coleman's men who defended the Confederate rear. Their gallant defense bought time for Morgan's column to attempt a crossing at Cheshire.

It was not meant to be. As the first raiders swam their horses into the Ohio River, a steamboat reared its ugly head around a bend from the north. It was the *Condor*, a transport boat assisting the Union navy. The Confederates did not know this fact; they assumed the vessel was a gunboat. Having dealt with gunboats much too often over the past two days, Morgan did not wish to investigate. He ordered his men to about-face, head inland about a mile and then turn south along the high road leading to Addison. Somehow, Coleman's troopers received no word about this change of direction. They continued into Cheshire, exhausted and hungry from their afternoon of skirmishing.

Shortly after Coleman's men entered Cheshire about 2:00 p.m. on July 20, Colonel Wolford's Union cavalry came up on them again. The Forty-fifth Ohio (Mounted) Infantry renewed their attack against Coleman's column, which wavered at the bank of the swollen Ohio River while the menacing *Condor* hovered nearby. The bewildered raiders fled south from

Confederate lieutenant colonel Cicero Coleman of the Eighth Kentucky Cavalry. His men's determined stand at Cheshire, Ohio, allowed Morgan and seven hundred raiders to escape capture on July 20. *Courtesy of Cowan's Auctions Inc., Cincinnati, Ohio.*

Cheshire with Wolford in hot pursuit, but they used the Stagecoach Road instead of the high road that Morgan had followed earlier. Captain Thomas M. Coombs, who was riding with Coleman, wrote, "Confusion took the place of order, and Officers could not control the men, and thus every man for himself, we again commenced to retreat down the river. In the confusion, the general part of Duke's and Cluke's regiments became separated from the rest of the command."

Instead of joining the main column, Coleman's group of about eighty officers and men turned on the Forty-fifth Ohio. After the raiders crossed the Stagecoach Road covered bridge over Kyger Creek, they noticed a rail fence ran diagonally from the bridge and across Coal Hill. It was an inviting spot to make a stand. They rode up Coal Hill for three hundred yards, dismounted, hitched their horses in the woods, marched back to the fence and concealed themselves in the fence corners where bushes and briars had grown.

The Confederates fired a volley at the Forty-fifth Ohio as it galloped across the bridge, sending the Union cavalrymen reeling back to the opposite side of the creek. When the raiders fired on the Buckeyes, Captain Lorenzo D. Hockersmith recalled that "it seemed as if one great big gun had been turned loose on the enemy. The surprise to the enemy was so great and so complete that the whole of the attacking command was for the time being completely at a loss to know what to do." Hockersmith believed that if the Rebels would have had fifty men on either side of the bridge, they could have captured Wolford and his men. But the Confederates didn't, and they had just fired their last round of ammunition.

Coleman's gallant band held the bridge for almost an hour until Colonel Adams's First Kentucky (U.S.) Cavalry and Captain Ward's company of the Third Kentucky (U.S.) Cavalry outflanked the right of the Confederate line

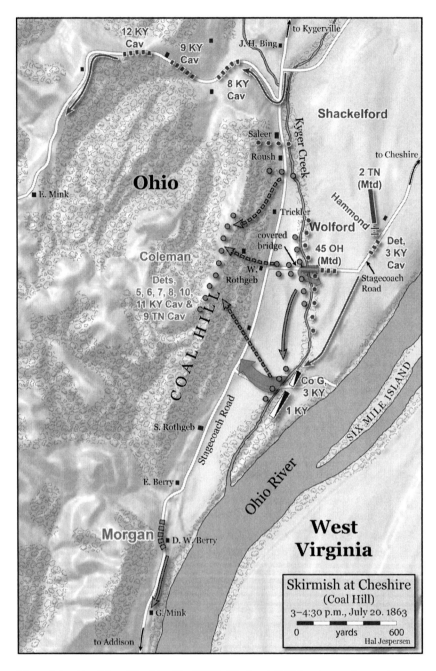

Map of the skirmish at Cheshire (Coal Hill). The battlefield lies three miles southwest of the town of Cheshire, Ohio. *Author's collection.*

and took possession of the Stagecoach Road about a half mile southwest of the bridge. This movement blocked the raiders' only escape route. To avoid being crushed between the two Union cavalry lines, the raiders retreated to their horses, mounted up and climbed to the crest of precipitous Coal Hill. There, Coleman reformed his line.

Meanwhile, the rest of Shackelford's troops followed a narrow wagon path in the rear of Coleman's position to complete the encirclement. About 4:30 p.m., Shackelford sent a flag of truce to Morgan demanding his immediate and unconditional surrender. Making their way down Coal Hill to the Wesley Rothgeb house, Coleman, Hockersmith, McCreary and other officers requested a personal conference with Shackelford to discuss the proposed terms. The terms allowed field officers to retain their sidearms and horses, and all others could keep their private property. Shackelford allowed them forty minutes to decide whether to give up or fight. Coleman held a council of war with Coombs, McCreary, Hockersmith, Joseph Tucker and the other officers. With their men exhausted, out of ammunition and surrounded, they had no other choice but to surrender their command. "All voted to surrender, and thus ended the saddest day of my life," recalled Major James B. McCreary, Eleventh Kentucky. Only a few men from both sides were wounded during the skirmish.

Although Shackelford later claimed he captured one thousand men at Cheshire, in reality only eighty Confederate prisoners were taken. Shackelford may have inflated the numbers to hide his embarrassment for allowing Morgan and most of his men to escape yet again. Shackelford reported that Morgan had been on the battlefield and had escaped under the flag of truce. It was claimed that even the Confederate officers believed Morgan and the other seven hundred men were included in the surrender. However, Morgan was riding near Addison at the time of the skirmish and may not have known about the rear-guard stand until it was too late.

Shackelford's victorious, worn-out troopers spent the night in Cheshire and in the fields west of town. Colonel Kautz's brigade arrived to reinforce Shackelford's contingent. Wolford and his men, including the "Wild Riders" of the First Kentucky (U.S.) Cavalry, were assigned to guard the prisoners. Out of respect for their fellow Kentuckians, they provided food to the famished Confederates.

Morgan turned his group inland again and marched north into the hills of southeastern Ohio. His strung-out column camped for the night around Porter. With morale in the division at its lowest ebb, about one hundred of the raiders left camp during the night and tried to make their own escape.

An 1864 photograph of Confederate officers incarcerated at Fort Delaware. Among them are ones who rode with Morgan. *Position from top row, left*: 4) Lieutenant Colonel Cicero Coleman, 5) Colonel R.C. Morgan, 6) Captain Charlton H. Morgan, 7) Colonel Basil Duke. *Position from middle row, left*: 1) Lieutenant Colonel Joseph Tucker, 6) Colonel W.W. Ward. *Courtesy of Hunt-Morgan House Deposit, University of Kentucky.*

They successfully wound their way south to Rankin's Point, but there they ran into a militia unit who captured the whole bunch before they could cross the Ohio River.

The next morning, as Morgan continued northwest toward Ewington, Shackelford gathered his men together at Cheshire. The determined Union general called for one thousand men and their best horses to volunteer to hunt down Morgan's band once and for all. Shackelford wanted men who "would stay in their saddles as long as he would, without eating or sleeping until they captured Morgan." Almost all the cavalrymen volunteered, but not enough serviceable horses were available. Even after Judah's cavalry cantered into Cheshire later that day, only five hundred mounts could be found that were strong enough to be ridden for great distances. Shackelford prepared a mixed group of five hundred volunteers for the long ride ahead, and at dawn on July 22, they rode off in the direction of McArthur, the last known place where Morgan had been seen.

Provisional Cavalry Division, XXIII Corps (July 22–26, 1863)* Brig. Gen. James M. Shackelford	
First Brigade (Brig. Gen. James M. Shackelford)	Second Brigade Col. Frank L. Wolford
14th Illinois Cavalry (detachment) Col. Horace Capron	2nd Ohio Cavalry (detachment) Capt. William H. Ulrey
5th Indiana Cavalry [90th Indiana Regiment] (detachment) Capt. Powers	1st Kentucky (U.S.) Cavalry (detachment) Adjutant William D. Carpenter
3rd Kentucky (U.S.) Cavalry (Co. G "Twyman's Scouts") Capt. Edward W. Ward	2nd East Tennessee (Mounted) Infantry (detachment) Maj. Daniel A. Carpenter
	45th Ohio (Mounted) Infantry (detachment) Lt. Col. George E. Ross

*Note: Other regular units would join the division on or after July 24. Among them were the 3rd Ohio (Mounted) Infantry (2 cos.), Captain Albert B. Dod; 86th Ohio (Mounted) Infantry (7 cos.), Col. Wilson C. Lemert; and three 6-pounder 3.67-inch brass howitzers of the 22nd Ohio Independent Battery Light Artillery, Captain Henry M. Neil.

Morgan's troopers rode to Ewington on the morning of July 21 and surprised 250 militiamen under the command of Lieutenant Colonel Louis Sontag. Sontag surrendered his troops without a shot and gave up his brand-new French rifled muskets with ammunition. These items the Confederates badly needed, since many of the men had lost their weapons during the flight from Buffington Island. Morgan paroled Sontag and his troops. Before leaving, Morgan gave his raiders the option of surrendering to the unarmed Colonel Sontag if they felt they could not or wished not to continue the journey with Morgan as their leader. Sontag promised to treat them properly. Only 54 men stepped forward to accept the offer. These raiders gave their guns, equipment and horses to their comrades, and then they marched away as prisoners with their unarmed foes.

Later in the day, the raiders captured and paroled Major Slain and two hundred militiamen who were coming to Sontag's aid. The Rebel column pushed on through the coalfields and forests east of Buckeye Furnace, passing through Iron Valley Furnace around dinnertime. At Vinton Station, they coaxed Vinton Furnace manager Isaac Brown to guide them northward. To keep McArthur from being pillaged, Brown tricked the raiders into taking a side route around the town. They eventually reached Creola about 1:00 a.m. on July 22, when they rested for a few hours while the Karns family served them food from a big iron kettle over an outdoor fire.

Turning northeast, Morgan led his men through Ohio's iron furnace region to the vibrant town of Nelsonville, which lay along the Hocking Canal. Here, Morgan's men replenished their supplies and horses. They also broke into stores and confiscated food from the residents. Before departing toward the northeast, the raiders burned ten canalboats and several bridges spanning the Hocking River and the canal. After a long day in the saddle, the raiders stopped for the night at the Weaver farm five miles southwest of Eagleport. While Susanna Weaver baked biscuits and grilled pancakes all night for the raiders, General Morgan took a nap on a straw mattress he had laid on her cabin floor. He and his men needed all the rest they could get. They would cross the Muskingum River at Eagleport in the morning.

Shackelford's Federal troopers filed into Nelsonville six hours after the Confederates had left town. After being treated to a bountiful meal prepared by the ladies, the indomitable cavalrymen carried on their pursuit, spending the night of July 22 in Millertown, less than ten miles in Morgan's rear.

At dawn on July 23, Lieutenant Colonel Robert W. McFarland and five companies of the newly organized Eighty-sixth Ohio Infantry marched to Zanesville's riverboat landing to board the steamer *Dime*. The steamboat and its special passengers sailed south on the Muskingum River, knowing well that Morgan's crew was somewhere between them and Marietta. They planned to intercept the raiders before they could cross the river. McFarland's four hundred greenhorns were anxious to have their first taste of war.

Meanwhile, with Mr. Weaver impressed as a guide, Morgan's 550 troopers rode northeast and reached the mouth of Island Run below Eagleport just before 8:00 a.m. The Confederate force split at this point. The head of the column followed the Muskingum River into Eagleport, while the rear of the column turned south to a position opposite the McElhiney house. Morgan deployed skirmishers along the west bank of the Muskingum to cover the crossings they intended to use.

Suddenly, shots rang out from the east bank of the river. Hidden behind bushes, trees and houses were several hundred young boys and old men of the Morgan County Militia, most of whom hailed from the immediate neighborhood. They were armed mostly with squirrel guns, shotguns and old flintlock rifles. Others carried pistols from the pre–Civil War days. Their shots struck a handful of raiders, including the Second Kentucky's Private Tommy Milton McGee, who fell mortally wounded. However, the majority of the militiamen's shooting was merely an annoyance, since their outdated guns lacked range and accuracy.

One grievously wounded raider was carried to a house in Eagleport, where he was left behind to recover. A young girl named Rachel Tignor was smitten by the handsome raider. She brought delicacies to him as he healed. "I'll bet you," Rachel later recounted, "that he was the prettiest man you ever saw!" Union authorities took the soldier away to prison when he was healthy enough to move.

While the farmers popped off shots at the raiders, Morgan's skirmishers returned fire. The raiders' more accurate rifles laid down a good cover fire, causing the militia's musketry to dwindle. Bullets riddled the town's structures, including the Weber and McElhiney houses, forcing their occupants to evacuate amidst a hail of lead. A Confederate bullet entered the window of the Weber house and barely missed Mrs. Weber (Weaver), who was performing housework when the skirmish erupted. "But they [the militia] stood in our door and fired on them," Lib Weber wrote two days later. "In an instant, the bullets were flying back here. There were four or five that went through the house. They made us all go back in the yard. You never saw people so scared in your life. We thought it was not safe to stay here, so we started for the woods."

Morgan arranged for a citizen to show his men the ford at the head of an island about 150 yards downstream of the dam at Rokeby Lock. Captain Virgil Pendleton, Company D, Eighth Kentucky, forced Johnny Fouts to cross and recross in order to prove the ford existed. Immediately, a column of cavalrymen rode their horses across the ford under the cover fire of their comrades, while another column of raiders swam their horses through the water a little upstream of the Richard McElhiney house. At the same time, a group of Morgan's scouts requisitioned Hiram Winchell's ferry in the village of Eagleport. They pointed their guns at Winchell as he pushed off. One raider exchanged his old kepi for the ferryman's newer hat. While the flatboat floated toward the village of Rokeby Lock, a dozen or more squirrel rifles popped, but none of the shots did any damage. The scouts

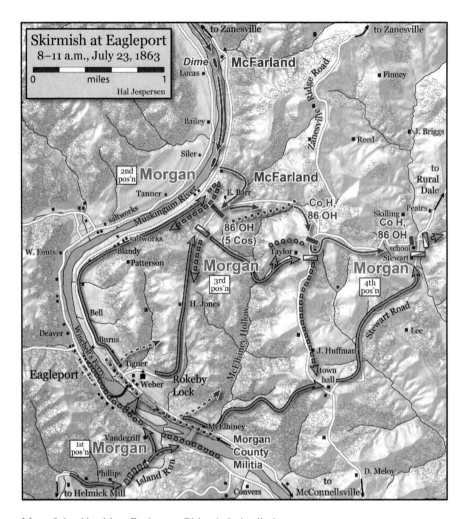

Map of the skirmish at Eagleport, Ohio. *Author's collection.*

quickly disembarked on the eastern shore. As the Rebel horsemen at the ferry landing and the ford swarmed up the bank, the militiamen at Rokeby Lock panicked and ran for the safety of the hills. The raiders galloped south on the river road and charged into the right flank of the militiamen posted around the McElhiney farm. The citizen volunteers released a round before they broke for McElhiney Hollow. The river was clear of enemy troops.

By 9:00 a.m., the rest of Morgan's troopers began fording or ferrying over the Muskingum from Eagleport to Rokeby Lock. Morgan sent his scouts out for several miles on all the roads leading from Rokeby Lock. Within an hour, the rear guard prepared to cross. General Morgan led his main column up the river road to Zanesville. In two miles, a disturbing message came back indicating that a steamboat—perhaps a gunboat—had been spotted around the bend ahead. It was the *Dime*. Memories of Buffington Island and Cheshire filled Morgan's head. He quickly ordered his column to about-face to Rokeby Lock. A scout directed them on an alternate road that took them up the river bluffs to the Zanesville Ridge Road, which would lead them north as desired.

McFarland's spotters saw Morgan's troopers turning around on the river road. The lieutenant colonel rightly deduced that Morgan would attempt to go north on the Zanesville Ridge Road. McFarland also knew a way to foil the raiders in their attempt. He directed the steamboat to land at the mouth of a deep ravine that led up to the Eli Barr farm. The tall river hills hid McFarland's movement from the raiders. The bluecoats quickly filed off the boat and scaled the steep bluff to the Barr farm only three hundred yards away.

The Eighty-sixth Ohio infantrymen reached the top of the ridge behind the Barr house well before Morgan's vanguard appeared on the road. The Yankees deployed into a line across the road on a low knoll, secreting themselves behind fences and bushes to hide their presence. As Morgan's troopers drew near, a nervous infantryman fired his rifle too early, alerting the Rebels of the Union position. McFarland's soldiers sent a volley in the direction of the Confederate column, but it was too far away to have much effect.

Morgan peeled away about one hundred of his men from the head of the column to engage the Union infantry, while he faced the rest of his men to the rear and led them back to Rokeby Lock for a second time. The head of the column exchanged shots with McFarland's foot soldiers until Morgan's rear had disappeared down the road. At that time, the one hundred raiders remounted and rode into a deep wooded ravine to the east. As the horsemen skillfully negotiated the steep slopes of McElhiney Hollow, the infantrymen watched in amazement.

McFarland ordered his left-flank officer, Captain Erastus W. Briggs of Company H, to march his men to the Zanesville Ridge Road in an attempt to head off the raiders. Briggs force-marched his soldiers to the intersection just ahead of the Confederate riders. The Ohioans opened fire on the Confederates, who had formed a thin skirmish line on Taylor's Hill opposite McFarland's troops. The volley tore into the Rebels' flank, and they immediately remounted and galloped south along the Zanesville Ridge Road. Briggs's company followed the tail of the Confederate column for a distance before the captain noticed that the Confederates were again riding north, this time on Stewart Road off to the left. Briggs turned his company around to head them off at the Stewart house.

Meanwhile, General Morgan reached Rokeby Lock, where all of his men were now standing safely on the east side of the river. A scout told him that a large body of Union troops—Colonel Joseph Hill's five hundred militiamen and two Nineteenth Ohio Battery pieces from Marietta—was closing in on Rokeby Lock on two separate roads. There were no other roads that led up the high river bluff. However, a narrow cow path had been discovered in the hollow behind the McElhiney house. General Morgan chose to use it. He and his cavalrymen showed off their excellent horsemanship as they scaled the steep wall of McElhiney Hollow to the intersection of the Zanesville Ridge Road and Stewart Road. Tom Webber described the slope as a "mountain side, up which nobody but a Morgan man could have carried a horse." They followed the Confederate vanguard in their quest to beat the persistent men of the Eighty-sixth Ohio to the intersection with the Rural Dale Road.

The third time worked like a charm. Morgan's advance troopers reached the intersection just before Briggs's Buckeyes. The Union infantrymen formed a line next to a schoolhouse a few yards distant from the intersection. They let loose a volley into the Confederate column, which reeled back for a moment before returning fire. Bullets flew between the opposing forces. Some of the projectiles embedded themselves into the walls of the Stewart house. Morgan pushed his men through the intersection. Their swift horses easily outdistanced the winded foot soldiers. Once again, Morgan had managed to find a way to escape, losing one man killed and ten wounded in the process.

Morgan led his contingent of over five hundred men on a night march. They rode around Rural Dale, passed through Cumberland and continued on to Senecaville. They foraged for horses, supplies and food in order to keep ahead of Shackelford's tenacious bluecoats. At Senecaville, Morgan knocked at the door of a milliner whose husband was away at war. Before the husband had left to join the Union army, he had given his wife a pistol to use if trouble ever presented itself at her doorstep. When she saw General Morgan outside the door, she pulled the pistol out of a drawer and aimed it at him through the blinded window. Before pulling the trigger, she imagined how terrible it would be if she were to learn of her husband's death at the hands of a Southern woman. She put the pistol aside. After opening the door, Morgan asked her directions to Campbell's Station. She and the general exchanged a polite conversation, at the end of which she confessed

A romanticized depiction of Morgan's entry into Washington, Ohio, published in *Harper's Weekly*, August 15, 1863. The view looks eastward. *Author's collection.*

that she had come close to shooting him. Deeply moved, Morgan smiled and said, "Do you know why you did not shoot? At that very moment Mrs. Morgan, at our home in Tennessee, was down on her knees praying for my safety. I am sure she was; several times in the past I have been as near death as I was a few minutes ago and on my return home, I would learn that Mrs. Morgan was on her knees praying for me at that very moment."

About 4:00 a.m. on July 24, Morgan and his troops entered Campbell's Station, a railroad town on the Central Ohio Railroad. The railroad, which connected Columbus with Wheeling, served as a major transportation route for the Federals to ship troops and supplies between the two theaters of the war. The raiders went to work burning railroad cars and buildings, tearing up tracks and destroying the Leatherwood Creek Bridge. They also took $4,000 from the Adams Express Company safe. After completing their whirlwind of destruction, they moved on to Washington, Ohio, where they arrived at about 8:00 a.m. Morgan went to the American House Hotel for a nap, while his men kept busy trading horses, raiding stores and confiscating food from the civilians.

Morgan's delay at Campbell's Station bought time for General Shackelford's men to close the gap with the raiders. The bluecoats entered the smoldering ruins of the railroad town about 9:30 a.m. After hearing that Morgan's troopers had departed less than two hours earlier, Shackelford sent his advance guard ahead with all possible speed.

About 11:00 a.m., a warning shot rang out. Shackelford was near! Rudely awakened from their naps, General Morgan and his staff ran down the stairs of the American House and scrambled to their horses. They could see Shackelford's advance guard forming a line on top of Cemetery Hill. The raiders quickly jumped on their horses and rode away on the Winchester Road.

A detachment of the "Wild Riders" of the First Kentucky (U.S.) Cavalry and Twyman's Scouts of Company G, Third Kentucky (U.S.) Cavalry, were the first to arrive on the scene. These battle-hardened veterans immediately opened fire on Morgan's retreating column. The raiders returned the fire as they stampeded through the streets. The bullets flew fast and thick across the town, crashing through windows of homes and businesses, forcing the citizens to seek shelter. "Women were screaming and children crying," remembered sixteen-year-old Elizabeth McMullin. "The shooting increased. Above the noise of battle we could hear voices coming from the Federal lines, ordering women and children to run to cellars. I ran into one that was nearest, where twenty or thirty women and other persons soon gathered."

When the firing ceased, the citizens emerged from their hiding places. Union cavalrymen galloped through the streets following their foe's trail. A few soldiers coaxed eight captured Confederates toward the old academy building, where they would be held before transport to a Cambridge jail. Two dead Rebels and several wounded lay in the streets. The townspeople would bury three of Morgan's raiders in the town cemetery and erect a gravestone in their memory.

A running skirmish continued for the next three miles. Just over the hill on the north side of Washington, the men from the Second Ohio Cavalry and Second East Tennessee (U.S.) Mounted Infantry pitched into Morgan's rear. The Ohioans dismounted, and a lively exchange of musketry ensued between the opposing forces. Sergeant Isaac Gause of Company E, Second Ohio Cavalry, participated in the fight:

> *The range was so short that the bullets sounded like yellow jackets. The grass was soon all cut away from around our feet by the shower of bullets that fell like so much hail. When the Second Tennessee dismounted and*

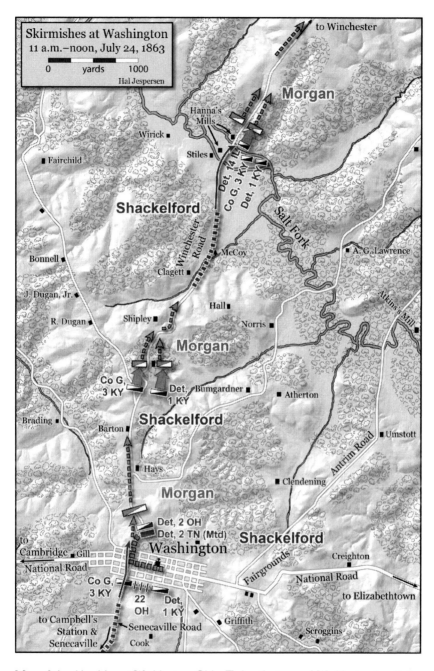

Map of the skirmishes at Washington, Ohio. Today, the town of Washington is called Old Washington, and Winchester is now named Winterset. *Author's collection.*

came over the hill in line, Morgan's men broke and ran. A volley that passed
over us was sent after them, but fell short of its mark.

A mile north of the town, along the southern fence line of the Archibald Shipley farm, Morgan's rear guard made a stand. Thick woods offered some protection for the boys in gray but did not stop the more numerous Federals from overlapping the Confederate line. The raiders departed after exchanging shots with the Union vanguard for a few minutes. Mr. Shipley's ox was the only casualty here.

Two more miles down the Winchester Road, General Morgan arranged a defensive line at the bridge over the Salt Fork adjacent to Hanna's Mills. He posted his men on a wooded hill on the north side of the creek and then had his troopers pull up the planks of the bridge so that Shackelford's cavalrymen could not use it. They waited for the Wild Riders and Twyman's Scouts to appear.

The raiders did not have long to wait. The Union advance filed into a field opposite Morgan's left flank. A detachment of Colonel Capron's Fourteenth Illinois Cavalry came up in support. At Shackelford's command, the Illinoisans forded the creek above the bridge and dismounted. While enduring a heavy fire from Morgan's troopers, Capron's cavalrymen advanced steadily up the wooded hill, driving the raiders before them. Morgan's men retreated to Winchester to rejoin the main column, which had gained some ground from the series of skirmishes north of Washington.

Shackelford's cavalry horses were breaking down in bunches, and his men were showing signs of serious fatigue. The lack of horses to replace their jaded mounts began to slow the Federal cavalrymen's progress. Sergeant Gause recalled losing his horse that he had ridden from Kentucky:

I had now a dreadful task to perform. I had to part with the most noble
animal it was ever my fortune to mount. Her limbs were trembling, and
every muscle quivered as the saddle was removed from where it had been
since last Sunday morning. When the decayed saddle-blanket, which had
been wet with rain and sweat for weeks, was removed, the skin came with
it, leaving the ribs bare. The underfolds fell to pieces, and I was able to
save only enough to keep the saddle from the back of my new mare. My
conscience hurt me for the treatment I had given my faithful animal, and I
dared not look at the poor thing. The tears rolled down my cheeks as I rode
away, telling the farmer to take good care of her. I assured him he would
not regret his labor.

Private Franklin Ackley, Company E, Second Ohio Cavalry. Ackley was typical of the hearty Union cavalrymen who chased Morgan for one thousand miles. *From Isaac Gause's* Four Years with Five Armies *(1908).*

Morgan took advantage of the skirmishes at Washington to increase the cushion between him and his pursuers. He sped northeast through Antrim and Londonderry before burning the covered bridge over the Stillwater River at Collinsport. The raiders plodded into Moorefield, where Morgan gave them a well-deserved four-hour rest. The general slept in the Mills Hotel while his men took their naps in the streets. Some of the raiders entered the abandoned home of Reverend Thomas Crawford. They found his sermon lying on a desk in the study. The raiders decided to have some fun. While one soldier read the sermon aloud, his comrades responded with a resounding "Amen! Amen!"

As Shackelford's vanguard drew near, the Confederate column departed Moorefield and headed for New Athens, a famous abolitionist town whose residents were in fear that Morgan's "terrible men" would burn the town in retribution. However, Morgan decided to bypass New Athens after learning from his scouts that a large militia force occupied the place. His guide led the raiders over an obscure path that passed through the dense woods on the west and north sides of town. About midnight, when they reached the Worley and Dickerson farms two miles northeast of New Athens, the exhausted raiders settled down for a short rest. At about the same time, Shackelford's vanguard limped into New Athens and encamped. The Federals had no idea Morgan's men were a hair's breadth away in the night.

Chapter 8

"Already Surrendered"

G eneral Burnside sat in his headquarters wondering how to stop Morgan. The pressure on the Union general was higher than ever. For over three weeks, the Rebel raider had managed to evade a vastly superior force of army regulars, home guards and navy personnel. President Lincoln anxiously inquired about Morgan's whereabouts, and then he followed up with a question about how soon Burnside could launch his invasion of East Tennessee. Burnside could do little about East Tennessee until Morgan and his band were caught.

Morgan held an advantage over his enemies whenever they tried to catch him by horse or on foot. However, the Civil War had introduced the use of railroads for conveying troops to the battlefield. Railroads would place Morgan's cavalry at a disadvantage.

Union major George Washington Rue turned thirty-five years old a month before he started on his journey to capture the wily Morgan. Standing at six feet, three inches tall, Rue was described as "stalwart" and "magnificent in physique." Raised on a farm in Harrodsburg, Kentucky, Rue fought with the Second Kentucky Infantry at Buena Vista, where he encountered John Hunt Morgan for the first time. Rue moved to Ohio in 1853 and settled in Hamilton. At the outbreak of the Civil War, he formed a company for Colonel Richard Jacob's Ninth Kentucky (U.S.) Cavalry and was named the company's captain in August 1862. He performed superbly in several cavalry skirmishes associated with Bragg's Kentucky Campaign, as well as in the monotonous scouting work along the Cumberland River, where he faced guerrillas like

Union major George W. Rue is widely recognized as the captor of John Hunt Morgan. After the war, Rue served as the first mail carrier in Hamilton, Ohio. He helped dedicate the Morgan surrender site monument in 1910. *Photo from Stephen Cone's* A Concise History of Hamilton, Ohio *(1901).*

Champ Ferguson. Rue understood Morgan's tactics, having spent most of the time since October 1862 chasing the Confederate raider around Kentucky. Rue rose to the rank of major by the start of the Indiana-Ohio Raid.

Rue participated in his regiment's fight at Marrowbone on July 2, 1863, but he became ill at the start of the ensuing chase and was bedridden in a Kentucky farmhouse for nearly two weeks. When he was strong enough to ride, Rue immediately took the first train to Cincinnati. There he reported to Major General Burnside, who placed him in temporary command of the Covington Barracks, located directly across the Ohio River from Cincinnati. During their interview at Burnside's headquarters, Rue suggested transporting cavalrymen and artillery by railroad to get in front of Morgan's command, which by that time roamed eastern Ohio. The railroad could also be used to quickly place Union troops between Morgan and the Ohio River. Burnside liked the idea, and he wanted Rue to lead the effort. Burnside ordered Rue to "take all the very best horses out of the thousand in the Covington Barracks, and mount every available man who could ride a horse." Rue gathered 375 veteran cavalrymen, equipped them with the best horses and firearms he had at his disposal and boarded them on a Little Miami Railroad train bound for Columbus on July 23. Burnside would use another recent invention—the telegraph—to inform Rue where to disembark his troopers from the train.

CAVALRY BRIGADE Maj. George W. Rue
1st, 9th, and 12th Kentucky (U.S.) Cavalry (detachments) (Maj. George W. Rue)
11th Kentucky (U.S.) Cavalry (detachment) Maj. Milton Graham
8th Michigan Cavalry (Cos. C, F, L and M) Lt. Nathan S. Boynton
15th Indiana Independent Battery Light Artillery Lieutenant William H. Torr (three 3-inch ordnance rifles)

Following Rue on another train from Cincinnati would be a small force of Michiganders under Major William B. Way. Way's contingent of approximately 250 men contained Companies C, D, E, H, I and K of his Ninth Michigan Cavalry and two rifled guns of Battery L, First Michigan Light Artillery (Eleventh Michigan Battery) under Lieutenant Thomas Gallagher. William Way came from Pontiac, Michigan. At the beginning of the war, he joined the First Michigan Cavalry as a lieutenant and served in the Eastern Theater, where he was promoted to captain for his bravery and skill in battle. In April 1863, he accepted the position of major for the newly formed Ninth Michigan Cavalry, which was sent to the West to contend with Morgan's raiders.

Morgan moved out before 4:00 a.m. on July 25 and took the road to Georgetown. With more men falling out of the column daily from sheer exhaustion, Morgan's force had dwindled to fewer than five hundred men. Scouts came back announcing the presence of a large body of militia on a hill southwest of Georgetown. Judge Samuel W. Bostwick and his one thousand Harrison County militiamen from Cadiz looked down on the Confederate column and prepared to fight. Morgan knew that Shackelford was close by, so he led his raiders on a detour up a steep hill on his right flank. As Morgan started over the hill, General Shackelford, whose men were traveling on a parallel road, caught sight of the enemy column in the distance. Shackelford quickly deployed Captain Henry Neil's Twenty-

Union major William B. Way ably led the Ninth Michigan Cavalry at the skirmish at Salineville, Ohio. He was promoted to lieutenant colonel in November 1863. In 1865, his brigade saved the Union cavalry from disaster at the Battle of Monroe's Crossroads, North Carolina. *Courtesy of the Library of Congress.*

second Ohio Battery, which opened fire on Morgan's men from long range. The artillery lobbed several rounds of shells among the raiders, wounding two of them before they disappeared over the hillside onto the road to Harrisville. Shackelford could not pursue immediately with his cavalry because his horses were in such bad condition and his men were so weary that they could not keep up with Morgan's pace.

Morgan entered Harrisville just before 7:00 a.m. on July 25. The men quickly raided the town of its supplies and horses. Harrisville's stores and shops received the same treatment from the raiders that many other towns in the North had been given over the last two weeks. The men also partook of the meals the local women had intended for Shackelford's men. Moving on, Morgan traveled east to Deyarmonville, located six miles from the Warrenton Ford on the Ohio River. Here his scouts told him the disappointing news that Union forces guarded the ford. Morgan had no other choice but to leapfrog his way north until he could find another crossing.

Awaiting Morgan at Smithfield was a small home guard unit under the command of Captain William Collins, who boasted of his military skills. A mile south of town, Collins's column was surrounded by Morgan's troopers before either one could fire a shot. The raiders quickly disarmed their enemy and exchanged their tired horses for the fresh ones among Collins's militiamen. Finally, they forced Captain Collins to ride a mule back into town while they sauntered along behind him. Upon entering town, Collins, under duress, told the citizens to feed these soldiers because they were Union men. The people of Smithfield happily obliged. Before the residents realized they had been tricked, Morgan and his troopers departed Smithfield with full bellies and fresh horses. What more could they have asked for?

Turning east toward the Ohio River, Morgan's troopers reached New Alexandria in the late morning. Again, scouts reported Union troops guarding the ford at Cox's Riffle four miles away. Morgan was incredulous but stubborn. He drove his men north through the rugged hills toward Wintersville, a small village located five miles west of Steubenville, the hometown of President Lincoln's secretary of war, Edwin Stanton.

On the night of July 24, Major General William T.H. Brooks, commanding the Department of the Monongahela at Pittsburgh, arrived in Steubenville with three regiments of trained Pennsylvania militia. He established his headquarters in the depot of the Cleveland & Pittsburgh Railroad, where he would conduct his operations against Morgan. Burnside had given him overall command of Union forces in the region. Brooks's first order of business was to send his regiments to guard various Ohio River fords above and below the city. Meanwhile, Major George W. Rue's 375 Federal cavalrymen arrived by rail at Mingo Junction. Rue reported to Brooks, who then ordered him to unload his troopers at Bellaire, where they would feed and water their horses until further orders were issued.

On the morning of July 25, Major William B. Way's Union force disembarked at the Mingo Junction railway station. Way reported to Brooks for orders. The general directed Way to unload his troopers and ride inland, leaving his artillery on the rail cars for later use. Way's cavalry departed toward the south, but when Brooks received reports that Morgan was heading north, Way countermarched and turned west on the road that passed between New Alexandria and Wintersville. At the same time, General Brooks sent Colonel James Collier's Steubenville Militia to Mingo Junction to support Way, but later he ordered Collier to return "speedily" to Steubenville and move west on the Cadiz–Steubenville Pike. Brooks hoped that Morgan's force would be caught between Way and Collier.

Colonel Collier's contingent consisted of five hundred mounted militiamen, including eighteen scouts under the command of Captain Frank Prentiss. An old six-pounder cannon accompanied the column. Collier sent Prentiss and his scouts ahead to see if they could make contact with the enemy. About 3:00 p.m., Prentiss spotted Morgan's column turning west onto the turnpike from the New Alexandria Road. Prentiss brazenly led his men to the western edge of Wintersville, where they poured their fire into the Rebel flank. Morgan's men were ready for them. They charged into Prentiss's squad and sent it reeling back through town. As the Union and

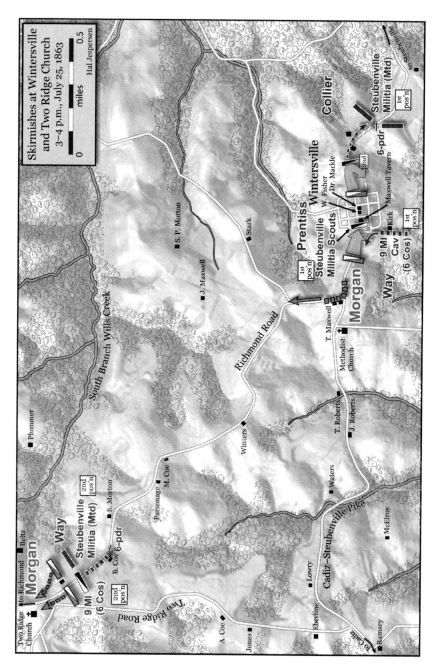

Map of the skirmishes at Wintersville, Ohio, and Two Ridge Church. *Author's collection.*

Confederate horsemen fought through the village, bullets struck various buildings. Earlier, the women of Wintersville had huddled together in the Maxwell Tavern to hide from the raiders. Now, they were in the center of the maelstrom. A stray bullet crashed through one of the windows and wounded Margaret Daugherty. The wound appeared to be mortal, but she would later recover. The frightened women quickly abandoned the tavern and ran through a gauntlet of lead to the safety of Dr. Markle's house.

Morgan's veterans easily drove off Prentiss's scouts, who lost sixteen-year-old Private Henry Park mortally wounded. Several of the scouts planned to run, but the captain dissuaded them when he threatened to shoot them if they tried. Prentiss reported back to Collier to hurry the rest of the Steubenville Militia forward. In the meantime, Morgan's raiders took advantage of the lull to break into stores and search for goods to their liking.

Some time had passed before Collier appeared on the hill east of town. He saw a large dust cloud on the New Alexandria Road on the west side of the village. Collier immediately unlimbered his six-pounder cannon loaded with scrap metal and unleashed it on the distant dust cloud. Pieces of metal flew in all directions, one fragment striking the Maxwell Tavern "with a resounding thwack," others planting themselves in the ground around the cavalrymen moving amidst the dust. Collier's gun continued to fire several rounds before an officer came riding out of the cloud with a white flag. "What are you fools shooting at?" inquired the officer. When he revealed he was a Union soldier from Major Way's command, and not one of Morgan's men, Collier was embarrassed. He had delayed Major Way's column for several precious minutes. Fortunately, no one had been hurt by the friendly fire.

Together, Major Way's six companies of the Ninth Michigan Cavalry and Colonel Collier's Steubenville Militia started after their common enemy. They caught up with Morgan's rear guard on the Richmond Road about two hundred yards south of Two Ridge Church. Collier set up his six-pounder gun next to the Benjamin Coe house while his mounted men formed a line farther ahead in support of Major Way's troopers. In the exchange of gunfire, a raider fell from his saddle wounded. The raiders quickly disengaged from the fight and dashed off toward Richmond. Two Michigan cavalrymen were also hit, including Private Martin Kane, who died from his wound and was buried in the Two Ridge Church cemetery.

Major Way halted at Two Ridge Church to wait for Lieutenant Gallagher's artillery to come up from Steubenville. The delay allowed Morgan to put more distance between his rear and Way. As the evening approached, the Michigander took his cavalry and artillery to a crossroads community known as The Eastern. There, he camped the night of July 25, barely a half mile away from Morgan's rear guard.

Meanwhile, the Confederates passed through Richmond at 5:00 p.m. and soon arrived in East Springfield, where they brushed aside a few home guards. Since their visit to New Athens, Morgan's men had experienced an increased frequency of attacks from home guards and militia, and it was starting to take a toll on the raiders. At East Springfield, a maiden lady named Miss Celia Davidson stubbornly resisted when the raiders tried to take her horse; they gave up the attempt. Bill Huskroff, a local farmer, was not so fortunate. When he offered to pay Morgan $400 in lieu of his horse, Morgan asked to see the money. When Bill pulled it out, Morgan took the money and the horse.

R. Mitchell Crabbs, a member of the Second Ohio Infantry, was on leave at the time Morgan's men visited his hometown. Without revealing his true identity, Crabbs befriended the raiders, and soon he began asking them questions. One soldier told him they were heading north to Babb's Island Ford near East Liverpool. As soon as the Confederates left town, Crabbs rode his swift horse along back roads to get ahead of the raiders. Crabbs arrived in Salineville about 10:00 p.m., at which time he wired General Brooks about Morgan's intended destination. This intelligence convinced Brooks to send Colonel Thomas F. Gallagher's Fifty-fourth Pennsylvania Militia by rail to Salineville later that night.

Morgan rode north to the mill town of Nebo, where he stopped for the evening at about 8:00 p.m. Morgan stayed at the Herdman Taylor house near the covered bridge over Yellow Creek. The Taylor women were required to cook chicken dinners for the general and his staff. Morgan's troopers spread out over the town and along the Monroeville Road for a couple miles. They lay down to try to get a little shuteye.

Union forces were closing in on Morgan's band from multiple sides. Major Way's vanguard camped only a mile south of Morgan's headquarters. At 10:00 p.m., Way sent a telegram to Shackelford informing him that he could take the direct road from Richmond to Hammondsville to get in front of Morgan's column while Way pushed the enemy from behind. Shackelford followed the advice. On the way to Hammondsville, he unexpectedly met Major George Rue and his Kentucky cavalrymen feeding their horses by the roadside. It was midnight, and Rue was getting ready to move on to Richmond. Earlier that day, General Brooks had ordered Rue up the railroad from Martins Ferry to Shanghai (McCoy's Station). From there, he had taken the road leading to the point where they stood. Reporting to Shackelford for orders, Rue asked to take the advance in the chase on the morrow. Shackelford told him to reverse his column and march to Hammondsville; there he would grant Rue's request. Both columns rode all night and rendezvoused at Hammondsville before 8:00 a.m. on July 26. From there, they turned northwest toward Salineville, with Rue in the lead.

Morgan was awakened on the morning of July 26 by a courier who said the advance had been attacked by Union cavalry scouts on the Monroeville Road. The general immediately formed his soldiers and led them north toward Monroeville, burning the Yellow Creek Bridge in their rear in hopes of delaying Way's troopers. It did not work. The creek was shallow enough to make it easy for Way's cavalry and artillery to ford the stream. Way's advance caught up and attacked Morgan's rear guard at Pott's School, and after a brief exchange of fire, the Union cavalrymen fell back. Morgan quickened the pace of his march. He reached Monroeville about 7:00 a.m., pausing only long enough to impress a guide named Jimmy Twiss, who would lead them to Salineville. Despite the raiders' need to keep moving, the Rebels managed to pilfer Potts Store before they scampered away to the north. Way's troopers were hot on their tail.

Just before 8:00 a.m., Morgan's scouts reached the curve in the Monroeville Road near the old mill in Salineville. Here they caught sight of Gallagher's Fifty-fourth Pennsylvania Militia regiment, which had arrived only two hours earlier. They also spotted Union cavalry approaching from the southeast. The scouts rushed back and reported the bad news to their general. Morgan was trapped.

Morgan decided to use his men's excellent horsemanship to his advantage. At the south end of the Burson farm on Morgan's left flank, a small path led down into a deep ravine to the west. He ordered Colonel Leroy Cluke, who commanded the rear guard, to form a line across the Monroeville–Salineville Road on the Burson farm and hold back Way's cavalrymen long enough for the rest of the raiders to escape into the ravine. Mounting his horse, Glencoe, General Morgan turned his column around and led it cross-country down the near-vertical side of the ravine. Horses slid down the slope, many falling and tumbling down with their riders. Other raiders were struck off their horses by tree branches. Amazingly, most of the column successfully negotiated the steep slope before Colonel Cluke's rear guard was violently attacked by Captain H.M. Rice and Company H, Ninth Michigan Cavalry.

Thirty-eight-year-old Roy Cluke hailed from Winchester, Kentucky. He enlisted in the cavalry in the summer of 1862, raised a regiment known as the "War Dogs" and was commissioned colonel of the Eighth Kentucky Cavalry of Morgan's command. Cluke's reputation as a hard fighter preceded him, but he was not a good disciplinarian. His men were known for being lax in their duties but tough in battle. Yet Cluke had proven himself as an independent

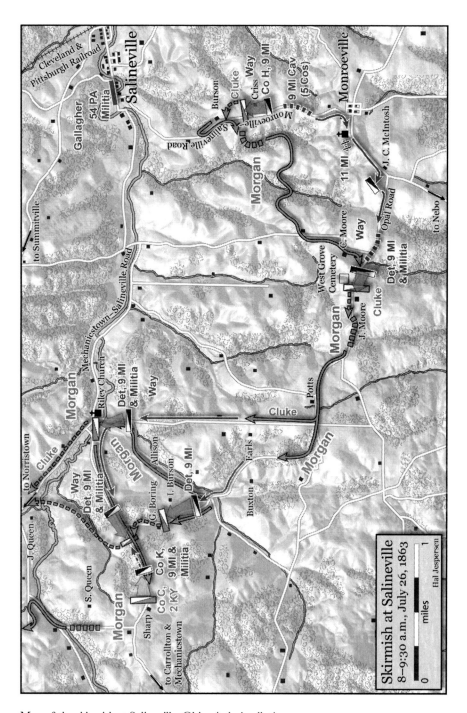

Map of the skirmish at Salineville, Ohio. *Author's collection.*

leader. From February through March 1863, he conducted his own successful raids on Union garrisons at Mount Vernon and Mount Sterling in Kentucky, for which he earned great praise from Morgan and Duke.

At Burson's farm, Cluke fought desperately for nearly a half hour before he saw the time had come to follow his commander into the ravine. As he withdrew his men down the slope, the Ninth Michigan charged. A brief but lively hand-to-hand mêlée ensued. The Union cavalrymen successfully surrounded fifty-five of Cluke's men and made them prisoners. Cluke left behind several wounded soldiers lying on the field at Burson's farm. Their opponent's wounded lay alongside them.

Rather than follow Morgan into the ravine, Major Way turned his troopers toward the rear and rushed them back through Monroeville. He intended to cut off Morgan's retreat before the Rebel chieftain was able to reach the Opal Road. As the Michiganders galloped through Monroeville, some local mounted militiamen joined them in the chase, which "now assumed the aspect of an old time fox hunt, with wily John Morgan playing the character of reynard."

Meanwhile, Lieutenant Tom Gallagher sighted the Confederate column coming south through the ravine toward his artillery's position in the Monroeville Cemetery. The rifled guns of the Eleventh Michigan Battery let loose, but their shells passed harmlessly over the heads of the Rebel cavalrymen. Gallagher realized the ravine was too deep. He could not depress his gun barrels enough to hit the raiders. Morgan veered west over the ridges and ravines to avoid the Union artillery.

The head of Way's column galloped by the McIntosh house and turned onto Opal Road. Some of the Federals stopped on McIntosh's Hill to fire on the raiders below them, but the Confederates were too far away to receive any damage. This poor choice delayed Way's troopers enough to allow Morgan to stay ahead of them. Morgan's column came out of the ravine onto the road leading south to the Cyrus Moore farm. Bullets were flying everywhere. From the Cyrus Moore house, the raiders headed west on Opal Road. Cluke's rear guard successfully gained the Opal Road just before Way's cavalrymen could attack them.

Morgan ordered Cluke to make another stand on the hill at West Grove Cemetery. From their position in the cemetery lane, the Confederates could see the oncoming Federal cavalrymen for several hundred yards. Cluke's men wheeled about, and as the Union vanguard galloped up the road toward them, the Confederates opened fire. Union saddles were emptied, but the determined cavalrymen kept coming. The raiders urged their horses to get away. Most men did, but a few did not. Many were captured, and several were

Confederate colonel Roy S. Cluke led the Eighth Kentucky Cavalry and took command of the Second Brigade at Reedsville, Ohio. After his capture, he was sent to Johnson's Island Prison, where he died of sickness in December 1863. *Painting from* Confederate Veteran Association of Kentucky *(1895).*

wounded. The Michigan troopers and militia struck down three of the raiders. Two of them would die of their wounds and would be buried by locals in the West Grove Cemetery, where they rest today. These two Confederates have the distinction of being interred on the northernmost Civil War battlefield east of the Mississippi River.

Cluke's gallant stand at West Grove Cemetery bought Morgan time to get away up the road to the Buxton and Boring farms. Cluke's men escaped on a different road leading directly north to Riley Church. He hoped to draw Way's cavalrymen away from the main column. Near the I. Burson farm, Morgan split his troopers to increase their speed. The lead group turned northeast in the direction of Riley Church, while the rear group headed north through the George Boring farm. While the head of the column passed the Allison farm, General Morgan made a pit stop at the house of Mrs. Keziah Morgan Allison, a distant cousin of John's. Before he left, she gave him a clean shirt and permitted some of his wounded men to stay under her care.

Way's troopers followed Cluke's trail as well as Morgan's trail. Way led his main column of the Ninth Michigan Cavalry and the militia toward Riley Church, where he struck the head of Morgan's column. While Cluke escaped north with the intent to rendezvous with Morgan near Norristown, General Morgan fought a short delaying action at Riley Church. As Major Way formed his men into a battle line, Morgan led his cavalry in the direction of Mechanicsville. Like Cluke had done previously for Morgan, now Morgan wished to draw Way's column away from Cluke. Way swallowed the bait.

Simultaneously, Way's rear guard struck Morgan's rear at the George Boring farm. In the skirmish that followed, several of the raiders fell wounded. The

Confederates broke for the Mechanicstown–Salineville Road, which they gained at the same time that Morgan's troopers from Riley Church passed them to the west. Morgan's rear guard was struck in the rear and flank by Way's converging columns, forcing the Confederates to leap the fence of the road and retreat through the fields of Jonah Queen's farm. Some of the raiders were captured, but others would successfully escape to rejoin Cluke at Norristown.

Morgan ordered one of his best fighters, Captain Ralph Sheldon, to dismount Company C, Second Kentucky Cavalry, for a rear guard action. Sheldon wheeled his "Old Regulars" about and placed them into line across the Mechanicstown–Salineville Road at the Sharp farm. In a few minutes, the bluecoats rumbled up the road toward them. Lieutenant Smith W. Fisk led the militiamen and Company K of Way's cavalry in the mounted charge. When Fisk's soldiers came within range, Sheldon's troopers unleashed a devastating volley on the Union horsemen. Men toppled from their horses. Confusion reigned. Lieutenant Fisk fell to the ground seriously wounded in the chest. Other Union cavalrymen and militiamen lay writhing in pain in the road. The survivors retreated to a worm fence in the woods two hundred yards to the east.

After a brisk skirmish with the dismounted Ninth Michigan and the militia, Captain Sheldon decided to charge the Union line. He mounted his company, and sounding the charge, they bounded toward the enemy line with pistols blazing. The Michigan troopers' Spencer rifles did nothing to stop Company C's attack. "Led by its gallant Captain Ralph Sheldon, one of the best of our *best* officers, this company dashed down upon the enemy," Duke recorded later. "The tired horses breasted the fence without being able to clear it, knocking off the top rails. But with their deadly revolvers our boys soon accomplished the mission upon which they were sent." The bluecoats scattered and ran down the road. Several of Sheldon's men were wounded in what would be the last fight of the raid. Leaving them in the care of the Sharp family, Sheldon withdrew his men toward Norristown. Way's men would not bother Morgan again.

Major Way's dispatches claimed he had killed twenty to thirty, wounded fifty and captured two hundred of the Confederates. However, in reality, only about one hundred raiders in total were killed, wounded or captured in the skirmishes around Salineville. The Federals failed to report their losses, but they likely amounted to fewer than twenty wounded between the regulars and the militia.

Morgan's column traveled north from the Sharp farm and rendezvoused with Colonel Cluke's men near Norristown. They learned from a guide that they could reach Babb's Island Ford or Smith's Ferry on the Ohio River by using the Beaver Creek Road leading from Hanover to West Point. The general decided to make another attempt to cross the river. Morgan and his troopers rode northeast between Bethesda Church and Summitville and gained the Beaver Creek Road at the Daniel S. McAllister farm. It was here that Morgan's raiders reached the northernmost point ever attained by a Confederate force from the contiguous Southern states.

Turning southeast, the raiders followed the valley of the West Fork of Beaver Creek. Beautiful farms adjoined both sides of the road. Before striking the intersection with the New Lisbon Road, the raiders captured a militiaman named Charles Maus, who told them a Union force lay up the road ahead. The Confederates soon encountered a barricade defended by a group of New Lisbon Militia armed with a small Revolutionary War cannon. The militia's commanders were Captain James M. Curry and Captain James Burbick.

When the green militiamen saw the Rebel column, most broke and ran for the rear without firing a shot. Morgan sent Maus with a flag of truce to Curry and Burbick. Morgan met with them to discuss the terms of their surrender. He offered to let them go if they agreed to lead him to Babb's Island Ford and ensure that his men got there without further interference from the militia. Curry and Burbick submitted to the terms, and Captain Burbick was selected to act as Morgan's guide. After the Rebel march had resumed, Morgan asked Captain Burbick to accept the surrender of his sick and wounded men. Burbick politely accepted.

When Rue and Shackelford reached Salineville, they received reports that Morgan was moving east along the Beaver Creek Road. Shackelford ordered Rue to take three hundred men and intercept the Confederate column. Rue rode away with the soldiers he had brought with him from Cincinnati. When his cavalrymen reached the Steubenville Pike, they turned north on it, hoping to cut off Morgan at its intersection with the Beaver Creek Road. Along the way, Rue picked up a local guide by the name of Dr. David Marquis, who was well acquainted with the area because of his frequent house calls.

Within two miles of the intersection of the Steubenville Pike with the Beaver Creek Road, Major Rue spotted a dust cloud. It was Morgan! Rue hurried his column forward, but when he was within a half mile of the intersection, Rue found that Morgan had already passed through it at a gallop. Dr. Marquis offered a shortcut. He pointed Rue to a nearby private farm lane that ran parallel to the Beaver Creek Road. The lane entered the dry creek bed about a half mile to the east and then struck the Beaver Creek Road at the Crubaugh farm in another half mile.

Rue saw his opportunity. He ordered a detachment of thirty men from the Eleventh Kentucky (U.S.) Cavalry to follow the Confederate rear while he led the rest on the shortcut to get in front of Morgan. They leaped off at a gallop. Without breaking their stride, the Union cavalrymen skillfully navigated the dry creek bed of the West Fork of Beaver Creek, crossed through some farm fields and gained the Beaver Creek Road about 150 yards ahead of Morgan's scouts. "I knew then I had him," remembered Rue. He immediately deployed his detachment into line of battle across the road at the David Crubaugh farm. He waited for Morgan to make the next move.

While topping a hill a half mile west of the Crubaugh farm, General Morgan spotted Rue's dust cloud toward the right and just ahead of him. The cloud seemed to inch closer to the Beaver Creek Road. Morgan realized then that he could not outmaneuver his pursuers any longer. He had traversed 586 miles of the Buckeye State and had avoided sixty thousand Ohio militiamen. But now his raiders were tired and demoralized. They were physically and mentally unable to cut their way out of this net.

Morgan had one more trick up his sleeve, however. He called to Captain Burbick and asked him if he would accept his surrender. Burbick, who was currently Morgan's prisoner, was initially flabbergasted by the question. Morgan said he would surrender to Burbick on condition that his men would be paroled, would be permitted to keep their sidearms and would be escorted safely out of the state. In a nagging tone, Morgan asked, "Will you accept my surrender?" Burbick replied, "Yes."

Minutes later, scouts reported to the general that the road ahead was blocked by Union regular cavalry. Morgan galloped to the front of the line to review the situation for himself. It was true. There was no escape this time. He sent forward Major Theophilus Steele, Charles Maus and two raiders with a flag of truce. Meanwhile, Morgan rode back a short distance to the David Burbick cabin, where he dismounted. He walked over to a nearby cherry tree in the Burbick orchard and sat down under its shade. It was a hot, sunny summer day. The tree's shade refreshed him as he waited for the Union commander's reply.

Rue was taken aback when Major Steele told him that Morgan demanded the Union commander's surrender. Rue replied that, on the contrary, he required Morgan's immediate and unconditional surrender or else be prepared to fight Major George Washington Rue of the Ninth Kentucky Cavalry. Steele returned to his lines and informed Morgan of Rue's demands. Morgan smiled and sent Steele back to tell Rue that Morgan had "already surrendered." But to whom? Rue requested an audience with the Rebel general, which was granted.

As Rue and his staff were escorted behind Confederate lines, he noticed large numbers of raiders spread out along the road fast asleep. They looked haggard and defeated. Rue met Morgan under the cherry tree near the David

Confederate major Theophilus Steele of the Seventh Kentucky Cavalry was a surgeon and one of Morgan's most trusted officers. Steele accompanied Morgan's white flag of surrender to Union lines near West Point, Ohio. He resumed practicing medicine after the war. *Courtesy of Cowan's Auctions Inc., Cincinnati, Ohio.*

Burbick cabin. They shook hands and exchanged pleasantries about the old days in the Mexican War. Morgan gave his Kentucky thoroughbred sorrel mare, Glencoe, to Major Rue for safekeeping. When a raider told him that Morgan had already surrendered to Captain James Burbick, Rue asked bluntly, "Who the hell is Burbick?" Burbick was a militia captain. After hearing this, Rue indicated he would not recognize any other surrender but one made to himself. Rue emphatically refused to honor the agreement that Morgan and Burbick had made. It was an arrangement made under duress and under no authority of the United States government. Looking around at his weary and downcast soldiers, Morgan had no options left. He surrendered to Major Rue about 2:00 p.m. Rue would hand Morgan over to Shackelford when he came up.

Within an hour, Shackelford and Wolford arrived from Salineville and surrounded Morgan's rear guard. The two leaders met with Morgan and Rue at the Burbick orchard to discuss the situation at hand. After a short debriefing, Morgan, Cluke and three staff members asked for a personal interview with Shackelford and Wolford. While Rue disarmed the prisoners, Morgan explained to Shackelford and Wolford that he had surrendered to Burbick and that the agreement should be honored. Shackelford called the agreement "not only absurd and ridiculous, but unfair and illegal." Shackelford went on to say that Morgan would be taken to departmental headquarters in Cincinnati where the Rebel general could take up his complaint with Major General Burnside. For now, at least, Morgan, Cluke, Webber, Owen and their men were prisoners of war. At 3:20 p.m., General Shackelford announced the news in a telegram to General Burnside: "By the blessing of Almighty God, I have

Boulder marking the traditional site of Morgan's surrender to Union major George W. Rue. This is the spot on the Crubaugh farm where Major Theophilus Steele met Rue to exchange terms under a flag of truce. Rue helped dedicate the monument on September 21, 1910. *Author's collection.*

succeeded in capturing General John H. Morgan, Colonel Cluke, and the balance of the command, amounting to about 400 prisoners."

The Great Raid was over. A total of 364 men and officers surrendered at the Burbick farm on July 26, 1863, only twelve miles short of the Pennsylvania state border. The traditional surrender site was marked with a large boulder on the Crubaugh farm at the spot where Major Steele and Major Rue first met each other under the flag of truce. However, Morgan officially surrendered to Rue, then later to Shackelford, under the cherry tree in Burbick's orchard. Morgan's men laid down their arms in the Crawford farm across the road. From there, Morgan and his raiders were escorted through Salineville to Wellsville, where they stayed the night. In the morning, they boarded trains bound for Cincinnati. They arrived to a huge crowd who had come out to catch a glimpse of the man who had caused so much trouble for so many people. The "Thunderbolt of the Confederacy" and his "terrible men" would not be creating any more trouble, at least for now.

Lightning War

G eneral Ambrose Burnside breathed a sigh of relief. With Morgan out of the way, the Union general could now begin implementing his plan to invade East Tennessee. He did so in September 1863, but the operation came three months too late—thanks to Morgan's Raid. By the time Burnside had captured Cumberland Gap and entered the Holston River Valley, the Battle of Chickamauga, Georgia, had been fought. Chickamauga was the largest battle in the Western Theater and the Confederacy's greatest victory west of the Appalachians. The battle helped lengthen the war in the West for another year. "Had Morgan been readily beaten back from Kentucky in a crippled condition, Burnside would have met Rosecrans at Chattanooga by the 20th of July; the battle at Chickamauga would not have been fought; and the war might have ended sooner," wrote Union colonel J.E. McGowan in retrospect.

On the other hand, Morgan's Indiana-Ohio Raid cost the Confederacy one of its best cavalry divisions. It also lost four artillery pieces and thousands of rifles and horses that the country would have a hard time replenishing. Most of all, the South no longer could count on the services of its favorite hero cavalier, John Hunt Morgan, who languished in the Ohio State Penitentiary with sixty-eight of his officers. They were treated like common criminals—like thieves, in fact. The rest of the captured raiders suffered in Northern POW camps such as Camp Douglas, Camp Morton, Camp Chase and Johnson's Island. Many of these soldiers would not survive the war.

Meanwhile, Colonel Adam R. Johnson worked hard to preserve the remnants of Morgan's Division. Only about 500 of the original 2,460 men who had started on the raid would return to the Confederacy. General Bragg tried to disband Morgan's Men and convert them to infantry, but Johnson successfully fought off Bragg's attempts. When Johnson nearly failed, Lieutenant General Nathan Bedford Forrest stepped in and saved the group by placing the remaining raiders under his wing. Forrest would do anything for a man he respected, and Morgan was one of those men.

True to his nature, John Morgan and six of his officers, including Thomas Hines, Ralph Sheldon, Samuel B. Taylor and Lorenzo Hockersmith, conducted a sensational escape from the Ohio State Penitentiary on the night of November 27, 1863. They reached the safety of Confederate lines before Christmas. Morgan received a hero's welcome throughout the Confederacy, but his desire to reform his former division never came to fruition. He received a new division of cavalry, but it would never attain the level of greatness like the one that left Tennessee in June 1863. During his last raid into Kentucky in June 1864, Morgan managed to capture his old adversary General Hobson at the Battle of Keller's Bridge, but the raid was tainted by excessive plundering that went well beyond the rules of war. The Confederate high command suspended Morgan and arranged a court of inquiry regarding his conduct. He would not live to defend himself. While stationed at Greeneville, Tennessee, his division was routed by a surprise Union attack. General Morgan was surrounded and shot in the back when he refused to obey an order to halt. The Confederacy's last cavalier died on September 4, 1864.

The sparkle of the Southern cavalry died with Morgan, but his impact on American military doctrine had only begun to be realized. The Indiana-Ohio Raid, though not understood by the great military men of his time, set a precedent for future generations of military planners. How could one man having fewer than 2,500 men with four cannons attract the undivided attention of nearly 130,000 enemy troops, inflict 6,500 casualties on them, cause nearly $1 million in damages on his foe and alter the strategic plans of an entire military department? How could a force of mounted infantry maintain a pace of forty miles a day in a period of a month and over a distance of nearly one thousand miles? How could such a small force penetrate deeper into enemy territory than any other incursion made from his nation? These were the questions that students of military history began asking themselves.

Did Morgan's Indiana-Ohio Raid change the outcome of the Civil War? No. Did the raid accomplish its mission: to divert Union troops away from Bragg's army? Yes. Raids cannot change the end result of a war. Raids are meant to help one side or the other in determining the outcome. Morgan's Raid did everything it set out to do and more. It helped a major Confederate army and boosted morale in the West when all seemed hopeless. More importantly, the raid forever changed the way war would be waged. Historian Don D. John observed that "the 'Blitzkrieg' of the German army and the speed and daring of General George Patton are to a great extent the mechanized development of Morgan's 'Lightning War,' a war of movement...Since the day of General Morgan, all cavalry tactics have been revised in warfare." Flora Simmons was right when she called Morgan's Great Raid "one of the most remarkable expeditions in military history."

Bibliography

Manuscripts

Cincinnati History Library and Archives, Cincinnati Museum Center, Cincinnati, Ohio:
    Roger Hannaford Papers.
    Thomas A. McCammon Papers.

Indiana State Historical Society, William H. Smith Memorial Library, Indianapolis, Indiana:
    Austin Family Papers.
    Thomas Johnson Civil War Memoir, 1880–1925.

Marietta College Library, Marietta, Ohio:
    William Rufus Putnam Jr. Civil War Collection.

Ohio Historical Society, State Archives Library, Columbus, Ohio:
    Charles W. Durling Civil War Diary. Transcript.
    Ford Family Letters.
    Nelson Banks Sisson Collection, 1840–1900s.
    Ohio Adjutant General's Papers.
    Records of the Military Committees of Gallia and Clermont Counties, July 14–23, 1863.
    Samuel C. Trescott Papers. Transcript.
    William Joslin Papers. Transcript.

Newspapers and Newsletters

Athens [Ohio] *Messenger*, 1863, 1872, 1930, 1931, 1953

Cadiz [Ohio] *Republican*, 1863

Cincinnati Daily Commercial, 1863

Cincinnati Daily Gazette, 1863, 1873

Cincinnati Daily Times, 1863

Cincinnati Enquirer, 1863, 1865, 1949

Cincinnati Times Star, 1933

Dearborn County [Indiana] *Register*, 1988

Democrat [Pomeroy, Ohio], 1927

Gallipolis [Ohio] *Daily Tribune*, 1863, 1932

Highland Weekly News [Hillsborough, Ohio], 1863

McArthur [Ohio] *Democrat*, 1863

Zanesville [Ohio] *Daily Courier*, 1863

Official Records and Publications

Dearborn County Auditor's Office. *Commissioners' Records of Dearborn County, Indiana.* Vols. 6, 7, 11. Lawrenceburg, IN: Dearborn County Auditor's Office, 1857–1872.

Hewett, Janet B., ed. *The Roster of Confederate Soldiers, 1861–1865.* 16 vols. Wilmington, NC: Broadfoot Publishing Co., 1995–1996.

———. *The Roster of Union Soldiers, 1861–1865.* 33 vols. Wilmington, NC: Broadfoot Publishing Co., 1997–2000.

———. *Supplement to the Official Records of the Union and Confederate Armies.* 100 vols. Wilmington, NC: Broadfoot Publishing Co., 1994–2001.

Holloway, W.R. *Documents of the General Assembly of Indiana at the Forty-third Regular Session, Begun on the Fifth of January, A.D. 1865.* Part 2. Indianapolis: W.R. Holloway, 1865.

Moore, Frank, ed. *The Rebellion Record: A Diary of American Events.* Vol. 7. New York: D. Van Nostrand, 1864.

Nevins, Richard. *Annual Report of the Adjutant and Inspector General to the Governor of the State of Ohio for the Year Ending December 31, 1863*. Columbus, OH: State Printer, 1864.

———. *Report of the Commissioners of Morgan Raid Claims to the Governor of the State of Ohio, Dec 15ᵗʰ, 1864*. Columbus, OH: State Printer, 1865.

Ohio Roster Commission. *Official Roster of the Soldiers of the State of Ohio in the War of the Rebellion, 1861–1866*. 12 vols. Akron, OH: Werner Co., 1886–1895.

Robertson, James I., Jr., ed. *The Medical and Surgical History of the Civil War*. 15 vols. Wilmington, NC: Broadfoot Publishing Co., 1990–1992.

Robertson, John. *Michigan in the War*. Lansing, MI: W.B. George & Co., 1882.

U.S. War Department. *The War of the Rebellion: A Compilation of the Official Records of the Union and Confederate Armies*. 128 vols. Washington, D.C.: Government Printing Office, 1880–1901.

Collected Letters, Diaries and Journals

Berlin, Jean V., and Brooks D. Simpson, eds. *Sherman's Civil War: Selected Correspondence of William T. Sherman, 1860–1865*. Chapel Hill: University of North Carolina Press, 1999.

Rosenburg, R.B., ed. *"For the Sake of My Country": The Diary of Col. W.W. Ward, 9ᵗʰ Tennessee Cavalry, Morgan's Brigade, C.S.A.* Murfreesboro, TN: Southern Heritage Press, 1992.

Tenney, Luman H. *War Diary of Luman Harris Tenney, 1861–1865*. Cleveland, OH: Evangelical Publishing House, 1914.

Williams, Charles Richard, ed. *The Diary and Letters of Rutherford B. Hayes, Nineteenth President of the United States*. Vol. 2, ch. 22. Columbus: Ohio State Archaeological and Historical Society, 1922.

Memoirs, Reminiscences and Regimental Histories Written by Participants

Admire, J.V. *Memoranda, Company E, 65th Regiment, Indiana Infantry Volunteers.* Osage City, KS: Osage City Free Press, 1888.

Allen, Theodore F. "In Pursuit of John Morgan." In *Sketches of War History, 1861–1865: Papers Read Before the Ohio Commandery of the Military Order of the Loyal Legion of the United States.* Vol. 5, edited by W.H. Chamberlin, A.M. Van Dyke and George A. Thayer, 223–42. Cincinnati, OH: Robert Clarke Co., 1903.

Ashburn, Joseph Nelson. *History of the Eighty-sixth Ohio Volunteer Infantry.* Cleveland, OH: A.S. Gilman Printing Co., 1909.

Berry, Thomas F. *Four Years with Morgan and Forrest.* Oklahoma City, OK: Harlow-Ratliff Co., 1914.

Chester, H.W. *Recollections of the War of the Rebellion: A Story of the 2nd Ohio Volunteer Cavalry, 1861–1865.* Edited by Alberta Adamson, Roger E. Bohn and Robert I. Girardi. Wheaton, IL: Wheaton History Center, 1996.

Duke, Basil W. *A History of Morgan's Cavalry.* Cincinnati, OH: Miami Printing and Publishing Co., 1867.

———. *Morgan's Cavalry.* New York: Neale Publishing Co., 1906.

Fifth Indiana Cavalry Association. *Fifth Annual Reunion of the Fifth Indiana Cavalry Association Held at Greenfield, Indiana, October 12 and 13, 1887.* Indianapolis, IN, 1887.

———. *Twenty-first Annual Reunion of the Fifth Indiana Cavalry Association Held at Portland, Indiana, October 14–15, 1903.* Greenfield, IN, 1903.

———. *Twenty-fourth Annual Reunion of the Fifth Indiana Cavalry Association Held at Greenfield, Indiana, September 12, 1906.* Michigantown, IN: Gem City Printing Co., 1906.

———. *Twenty-sixth Annual Reunion of the Fifth Indiana Cavalry Association Held at Rushville, Indiana, October 14–15, 1908.* Carmel, IN: Star Printers, 1909.

Fout, Frederick W. *The Dark Days of the Civil War, 1861 to 1865: The West Virginia Campaign of 1861, the Antietam and Harper's Ferry Campaign of 1862, the East Tennessee campaign of 1863, the Atlanta Campaign of 1864*. St. Louis, MO: F.A. Wagenfuehr, 1904.

Gause, Isaac. *Four Years with Five Armies: Army of the Frontier, Army of the Potomac, Army of the Missouri, Army of the Ohio, Army of the Shenandoah*. New York: Neale Publishing Co., 1908.

Hockersmith, L.D. *Morgan's Escape: A Thrilling Story of War Times, A True History of the Raid of General Morgan and His Men through Kentucky, Indiana and Ohio*. Madisonville, KY: Glenn's Graphic Print, 1903.

Johnson, Adam R. *The Partisan Rangers of the Confederate States Army*. Louisville, KY: George G. Fetter Co., 1904.

Logan, India W. Peddicord. *Kelion Franklin Peddicord of Quirk's Scouts, Morgan's Kentucky Cavalry, C.S.A.* New York: Neale Publishing Co., 1908.

McGowan, J.E. "Morgan's Indiana and Ohio Raid." In *The Annals of the War Written by Leading Participants North and South*. Edited by Alexander K. McClure, 750–69. Philadelphia: Times Publishing Company, 1879.

Porter, John M. *One of Morgan's Men: Memoirs of Lieutenant John M. Porter of the Ninth Kentucky Cavalry*. Edited by Kent Masterson Brown. Lexington: University Press of Kentucky, 2011.

Sammons, John H. *Personal Recollections of the Civil War*. Greensburg, IN: Montgomery & Son, n.d.

Sanford, Washington L. *History of Fourteenth Illinois Cavalry and the Brigades to Which It Belonged*. Chicago: R.R. Donnelley & Sons Co., 1898.

Smith, Sydney K. *Life, Army Record, and Public Services of D. Howard Smith*. Louisville, KY: Bradley & Gilbert, 1890.

Stone, Henry Lane. *"Morgan's Men"—A Narrative of Personal Experiences*. Louisville, KY: Westerfield-Bonte Co., 1919.

Tarrant, Sergeant E. *The Wild Riders of the First Kentucky Cavalry: A History of the Regiment in the Great War of the Rebellion, 1861–1865*. Louisville, KY: Press of R.H. Carothers, 1894.

Tracie, Theodore C. *Annals of the Nineteenth Ohio Battery Volunteer Artillery; Including an Outline of the Operations of the Second Division, Twenty-third Army Corps; Lights and Shadows of Army Life, As Seen on the March, Bivouac, and Battlefield*. Cleveland, OH: J.B. Savage, 1878.

Weaver, H.C. "Morgan's Raid in Kentucky, Indiana, and Ohio, July, 1863." In *Sketches of War History, 1861–1865: Papers Prepared for the Ohio Commandery of the Military Order of the Loyal Legion of the United States*. Vol. 4, edited by W.H. Chamberlin, 278–314. Cincinnati, OH: Robert Clarke Co., 1896.

Wormer, Grover S. "The Morgan Raid." In *War Papers Read Before the Michigan Commandery of the Military Order of the Loyal Legion of the United States*. Vol. 2, edited by the Michigan Commandery of the Loyal Legion of the United States, 191–216. Detroit, MI: James H. Stone & Co., 1898.

Young, Bennett H. *Confederate Wizards of the Saddle: Being Reminiscences and Observations of One Who Rode with Morgan*. Boston: Chapple Publishing Co., 1914.

Books and Maps

Austin, L.G. *Illustrated Historical and Business Review of Meigs and Gallia Counties, Ohio, for the Year 1891*. Springfield, IL: Union Publishing Co., 1891.

Badgley, C. Stephen. *The Battle of Buffington Island: A Look at Morgan's Dash Through Meigs County, Ohio in 1863*. Canal Winchester, OH: Badgley Publishing Co., 2011.

Battle, J.H., W.H. Perrin and G.C. Kniffin. *Kentucky: A History of the State*. 4th ed. Louisville, KY: F.A. Battey Publishing Company, 1887.

Blount, Jim. *The Civil War and Butler County*. Hamilton, OH: Past/Present/Press, 1998.

————. *Greenwood Biographies: A Hamilton Bicentennial Project of the Greenwood Cemetery Association.* Hamilton, OH: Greenwood Cemetery Association, 1991.

Bradley, Michael R. *Tullahoma: The 1863 Campaign for the Control of Middle Tennessee.* Shippensburg, PA: Burd Street Press, 2000.

Brant and Fuller. *History of Vanderburgh County, Indiana, from the Earliest Times to the Present, with Biographical Sketches, Reminiscences, etc.* Madison, WI: Brant & Fuller, 1889.

Brown, Dee Alexander. *Morgan's Raiders.* New York: Konecky & Konecky, 1959.

Burton, Katherine. *Three Generations: Maria Boyle Ewing (1801–1864); Ellen Ewing Sherman (1824–1888); Minnie Sherman Fitch (1851–1913).* New York: Longmans, Green & Co., 1947.

Cahill, Lora Schmidt. *The John Hunt Morgan Heritage Trail in Indiana: A Tour Guide to the Indiana Portion of Morgan's Great Raid, July 8–13, 1863.* Attica, OH: K-Hill Publications, 1997.

Cahill, Lora Schmidt, and David L. Mowery. *Morgan's Raid Across Ohio: The Civil War Guidebook of the John Hunt Morgan Heritage Trail.* Columbus: Ohio Historical Society, 2013.

Caldwell, J.A. *History of Belmont and Jefferson Counties, Ohio, and Incidentally Historical Collections Pertaining to Border Warfare and the Early Settlement of the Adjacent Portion of the Ohio Valley.* Wheeling, WV: Historical Publishing Co., 1880.

Cone, Stephen Decatur. *A Concise History of Hamilton, Ohio.* Middletown, OH: Press of George Mitchell, 1901.

Confederate Veteran Association of Kentucky. *Confederate Veteran Association of Kentucky: Constitution, By-Laws and List of Membership, Arranged by Counties, with Name, Rank, Residence and Command of Every Member in His Own County Camp, If One Has Been Organized, or in the John C. Breckinridge Camp.* 5th ed. Lexington, KY: Transylvania Printing Co., 1895.

Connelley, William Elsey, and Ellis Merton Coulter. *History of Kentucky.* 5 vols. Chicago: American Historical Society, 1922.

Corum, James S. *The Roots of Blitzkrieg: Hans von Seeckt and German Military Reform.* Lawrence: University Press of Kansas, 1992.

Cozzens, Peter. *No Better Place to Die: The Battle of Stones River.* Chicago: University of Illinois Press, 1991.

Crawford, Richard. *Lightning Across the River: The Story of Gen. John Hunt Morgan's Raid on Clermont County, Ohio; U.S. Grant: Clermont County's Most Noted Son.* Newport, KY: Rhiannon Publications, 1996.

Doyle, Joseph B. *20th Century History of Steubenville and Jefferson County, Ohio, and Representative Citizens.* Chicago: Richmond-Arnold Publishing Co., 1910.

Eckley, H.J., and W.T. Perry, eds. *History of Carroll and Harrison Counties, Ohio.* 2 vols. Chicago: Lewis Publishing Co., 1921.

Ervin, Robert Edgar. *The John Hunt Morgan Raid of 1863.* Jackson, OH: Robert E. Ervin, 2003.

Evans, Nelson W., and Emmons B. Stivers. *A History of Adams County, Ohio: From Its Earliest Settlement to the Present Time.* West Union, OH: E.B. Stivers, 1900.

Fuller, J.F.C. *Armored Warfare: An Annotated Edition of Lectures on F.S.R. III (Operations Between Mechanized Forces).* Harrisburg, PA: Military Service Publishing Co., 1943.

Gard, Ronald Max. *Morgan's Raid into Ohio.* Lisbon, OH: Lyle Printing & Publishing Co., 1963.

Gorin, Betty J. *"Morgan Is Coming!" Confederate Raiders in the Heartland of Kentucky.* Louisville, KY: Harmony House Publishers, 2006.

Hart, Basil Henry Liddell. *Strategy.* New York: Praeger, 1954.

Hayes, Eli L. *Illustrated Atlas of the Upper Ohio River and Valley from Pittsburgh, Pa. to Cincinnati, Ohio: From United States Official and Special Surveys.* Philadelphia: Titus, Simmons & Titus, 1877.

Hill, Agnes C. *Tuppers Plains and the Surrounding Area of Olive & Orange Townships: Stories and Pictures of the Yesterdays.* Tuppers Plains, OH: Agnes C. Hill, 1985.

BIBLIOGRAPHY

Holland, Cecil Fletcher. *Morgan and His Raiders: A Biography of the Confederate General.* New York: MacMillan Co., 1942.

Horwitz, Lester V. *The Longest Raid of the Civil War: Little-Known & Untold Stories of Morgan's Raid into Kentucky, Indiana & Ohio.* Cincinnati, OH: Farmcourt Publishing, 1999.

John, Don D., ed. *The Great Indiana-Ohio Raid by Brig.-Gen. John Hunt Morgan and His Men, July 1863.* Louisville, KY: Book Nook Press, 1955.

Kautz, Lawrence G. *August Valentine Kautz, U.S.A.: Biography of a Civil War General.* Jefferson, NC: McFarland & Co., 2008.

Keller, Alan. *Morgan's Raid.* New York: Collier Books, 1961.

Kjellenberg, Marion S. *History and Directory of Ole' Montgomery: 1795–1967.* Montgomery, OH: Marion S. Kjellenberg, 1967.

Longacre, Edward G. *Mounted Raids of the Civil War.* New York: A.S. Barnes and Co., 1975.

Mansfield, Edward Deering. *The Ohio Railroad Guide, Illustrated: Cincinnati to Erie via Columbus and Cleveland.* Columbus: Ohio State Journal Co., 1854.

Mathews, A.E. *View of Camp Dennison: 16 Miles Northeast of Cincinnati, Ohio.* Cincinnati, OH: Middleton, Strobridge & Co., 1865.

Matthews, Gary Robert. *Basil Wilson Duke, C.S.A.: The Right Man in the Right Place.* Lexington: University Press of Kentucky, 2005.

McGavran, S.B. *A Brief History of Harrison County, Ohio.* Cadiz, OH: Harrison Tribune, 1894.

Metzler, William E. *Morgan and His Dixie Cavaliers: A Biography of the Colorful Confederate General.* N.p.: William E. Metzler, 1976.

Mulesky, Raymond, Jr. *Thunder from a Clear Sky: Stovepipe Johnson's Confederate Raid on Newburgh, Indiana.* Lincoln, NE: iUniverse Star, 2006.

Nikazy, Eddie M. *Forgotten Soldiers: History of the 2nd Tennessee Volunteer Infantry Regiment (USA), 1861–1865*. Bowie, MD: Heritage Books, 1996.

Ogan, Lew. *History of Vinton County, Ohio: Wonderland of Ohio*. McArthur, OH, 1954.

Poole, Ann. *Deer Park: Past to Present*. Cincinnati, OH: V&L Offset Printing, 1987.

Power, Jim. *The "Iron Man" and the "Mississippi Company" of Morgan's Raiders*. Bloomington, IN: AuthorHouse, 2009.

Price, Gayle H. *Morgan's Raid and the Battle of Buffington Island*. Pomeroy, OH: Meigs County Historical Society, 1997.

Ramage, James A. *Rebel Raider: The Life of John Hunt Morgan*. Lexington: University Press of Kentucky, 1986.

Richmond, Robert N., ed. *How General John Hunt Morgan Invaded Morgan County, Ohio, 125 Years Ago—July 23, 1863: A 125th Anniversary Commemoration Booklet*. McConnelsville, OH: Morgan County Historical Society, 1988.

Robertson, Charles. *History of Morgan County, Ohio, with Portraits and Biographical Sketches of Some of Its Pioneers and Prominent Men*. Chicago: L.H. Watkins & Co., 1886.

Senour, F., Reverend. *Morgan and His Captors*. Cincinnati, OH: C.F. Vent & Co., 1865.

Simmons, Flora E. *A Complete Account of the John Morgan Raid through Kentucky, Indiana, and Ohio in July 1863*. Cincinnati, OH: Flora E. Simmons, 1863.

Simms, Jere H. *Last Day and Last Night of John Morgan's Raid*. East Liverpool, OH: Jere H. Simms, 1913.

Sloan, Mary R. *History of Camp Dennison, Ohio*. 3rd ed. Cincinnati, OH: Queen City Printing, 2003.

Smith, Myron J., Jr. *Le Roy Fitch: The Civil War Career of a Union River Gunboat Commander*. Jefferson, NC: McFarland & Company, 2007.

Southworth, Samuel A., ed. *Great Raids in History: From Drake to Desert One*. 1997. Reprint, Edison, NJ: Castle Books, 2002.

Stivers, Aaron. *Meigs County, Ohio: From Hardesty's Historical and Geographical Encyclopedia, 1883, and Property Owners as Shown by Map of Meigs County, c. 1867.* 1883. Reprint, Defiance, OH: Meigs County Pioneer and Historical Society, 1982.

Surby, Richard W. *Two Great Raids.* Washington, D.C.: National Tribune, 1897.

Symonds, Craig L. *A Battlefield Atlas of the Civil War.* 2nd ed. Baltimore, MD: Nautical and Aviation Publishing Company of America, 1983.

Warner, Ezra J. *Generals in Blue: Lives of the Union Commanders.* Baton Rouge: Louisiana State University Press, 1992.

————. *Generals in Gray: Lives of the Confederate Commanders.* Baton Rouge, LA: Louisiana State University Press, 1987.

Watkins, Elizabeth, and Dwight G. Watkins. *Morgan's Light Brigade: Brigadier John H. Morgan's Old Cavalry Division.* Utica, KY: McDowell Publications, 2001.

White, Julius. "Burnside's Occupation of East Tennessee." In *Military Essays and Recollections: Papers Read Before the Commandery of the State of Illinois, Military Order of the Loyal Legion of the United States.* Vol. 4, edited by the Illinois Commandery of the Loyal Legion of the United States, 301–02. Chicago: Cozzens & Beaton Co., 1907.

Williams & Company. *Williams' Cincinnati Directory, City Guide, & Business Mirror.* Cincinnati, OH: Williams & Co., 1863.

Williams, T. Harry. *Hayes of the Twenty-third: The Civil War Volunteer Officer.* New York: Alfred A. Knopf, 1965.

Wimberg, Robert J. *Cincinnati and the Civil War: Off to Battle.* Cincinnati: Ohio Book Store, 1992.

Wolfe, William G. *Stories of Guernsey County, Ohio: History of an Average Ohio County.* Cambridge: Ohio Genealogical Society, 1975.

Wyeth, John Allan. *That Devil Forrest: Life of General Nathan Bedford Forrest.* Baton Rouge: Louisiana State University Press, 1989.

Articles

Bennett, B. Kevin. "The General's Tour—Morgan's Luck Runs Out: The Battle of Buffington Island, July 19, 1863." *Blue and Gray Magazine* 15, no. 4 (Spring 1998): 6–20, 48–65.

Bennett, Pamela J., ed. "Curtis R. Burke's Civil War Journal." *Indiana Magazine of History* 65 (December 1969): 283–327.

Duke, Basil W., Thomas H. Hines and Orlando B. Willcox. "The Romance of Morgan's Rough Riders: The Raid, the Capture, and the Escape." *Century Magazine* (January 1891).

McCreary, James Bennett. "The Journal of My Soldier Life." *Register of the Kentucky State Historical Society* 33, no. 104 (July 1935): 191–211.

Miller, William Marion. "Major George W. Rue, the Captor of General John Morgan." *Ohio Historical Quarterly* 50 (April–June 1941): 130–34.

———. "An Unrecorded Incident of Morgan's Raid." *Ohio Historical Quarterly* 54 (April–June 1945): 169–70.

Ohio Historical Society. "John Morgan Raid in Ohio." *Ohio Archaeological and Historical Publications* 17 (January 1908): 48–59.

Quisenberry, A.C. "History of Morgan's Men." *Register of the Kentucky State Historical Society* 15, no. 45 (September 1917): 23–48.

Rue, George W. "Celebration of the Surrender of General John H. Morgan: An Account by Morgan's Captor, Major George W. Rue." *Ohio Historical Quarterly* 20 (October 1911): 368–77.

Smith, Myron Smith, Jr. "'I Will Cut Him Off at All Hazards': Le Roy Fitch Meets the 'Thunderbolt of the Confederacy'—Buffington Island, July 19, 1863." *North & South* 14, no. 3 (September 2012): 28–37.

Still, John S. "Blitzkrieg, 1863: Morgan's Raid and Rout." *Quarterly Journal of Studies in Civil War History* 3 (September 1957): 291–306.

Towne, Stephen E., and Jay G. Heiser. "'Everything Is Fair in War': The Civil War Memoir of George A. 'Lightning' Ellsworth, Telegraph Operator for John Hunt Morgan." *Register of the Kentucky State Historical Society* 108, nos. 1–2 (Winter/Spring 2010): 3–110.

Weber, L.J. "Morgan's Raid." *Ohio Archaeological and Historical Publications* 18 (January 1909): 79–104.

Unpublished Manuscripts

Mowery, David L. "A Study of John Hunt Morgan's Ohio Raid Route from Reedsville to Creola, Ohio, July 19–22, 1863." 2nd ed. Unpublished manuscript in possession of the Ohio Historical Society, State Archives Library, Columbus, Ohio, 2011.

Pratt, G. Michael. "The Battle of Buffington Island: The End of Morgan's Trail; A Report on the Archaeological Survey, American Battlefield Protection Program Grant No. GA-2255-99-013." Unpublished manuscript in the possession of the Center for Historic and Military Archaeology, Heidelberg College, Tiffin, OH, 2000.

Electronic Sources

Coombs, Thomas Monroe. "Diary of Captain Thomas Monroe Coombs, Co. C, 5th KY Cavalry CSA." Edited by Neil Allen Bristow. *Green Wolf Family History Pages*. http://freepages.genealogy.rootsweb.ancestry.com/~greenwolf/coombs/index.htm.

———. "Letter from Captain Thomas Monroe Coombs, Co. C, 5th KY Cavalry CSA, to his wife Lou, August 14–15, 1863." Edited by Neil Allen Bristow. *Green Wolf Family History Pages*. http://freepages.genealogy.rootsweb.ancestry.com/~greenwolf/coombs/letter.htm.

Bibliography

Ewing, George. "1863–07 Letter Fragment from George Ewing – July 1863." *Seeking Michigan, Civil War Manuscripts Collection Home Page.* http://seekingmichigan.org/wp-content/uploads/2009/08/630700-George-Ewing.pdf.

"The Great Raid, Summer 1863." *Trails-R-Us (Kentucky)—John Hunt Morgan Home Page.* http://www.trailsrus.com/morgan/map.html.

"Historic North America Regionial Map: Kentucky, Indiana, Ohio." *Historic Map Works: Residential Genealogy.* http://www.historicmapworks.com.

"Historic USGS Maps Collection (ca. 1900–1920)." *MyTopo Home Page.* http://maptech.mytopo.com/onlinemaps/index.cfm.

"United States Special Operations Command." In *Wikipedia: The Free Encyclopedia.* http://en.wikipedia.org/wiki/United_States_Special_Operations_Command.

Weatherred, John. "Wartime Diary of John Weatherred, Bennett's Regiment or 9th Tennessee Cavalry, John Hunt Morgan's Command." Edited by Jack Masters. *The Wartime Diary of John Weatherred.* http://www.jackmasters.net/9tncav.html.

Index

About the Author

David L. Mowery, a native resident of Cincinnati, Ohio, and a graduate of the University of Cincinnati, has lived at various points along the path of Morgan's Raid for most of his life. American military history piqued his interest at an early age. Since childhood, he has researched and visited over six hundred battlefields across fifty states and eight countries. In 2001, David joined the all-volunteer Ohio Civil War Trail Commission as its Hamilton County representative, but over the years his role expanded to include the final design and historical validation of the entire length of the John Hunt Morgan Heritage Trail of Ohio. He is the co-author of *Morgan's Raid Across Ohio: The Civil War Guidebook of the John Hunt Morgan Heritage Trail* (Ohio Historical Society, 2013) and the author of the thesis titled "A Study of John Hunt Morgan's Ohio Raid Route from Reedsville to Creola, Ohio, July 19–22, 1863" (Ohio Historical Society, 2011), the first comprehensive study of Morgan's whereabouts during the three controversial days following the Battle of Buffington Island. Since 1995, David has been a member of the Cincinnati Civil War Round Table, for which he has written various papers on Civil War subjects. He has also served with the Buffington Island Battlefield Preservation Foundation, the grass-roots organization working to preserve Ohio's only Civil War battlefield.

Visit us at
www.historypress.net